Bjørn Helland-Hansen

The Sea West of Spitsbergen

The Oceanographic Observations of the Isachsen Spitsbergen Expedition in

1910

Bjørn Helland-Hansen

The Sea West of Spitsbergen

The Oceanographic Observations of the Isachsen Spitsbergen Expedition in 1910

ISBN/EAN: 9783954272075
Erscheinungsjahr: 2012
Erscheinungsort: Bremen, Deutschland

© maritimepress in Europäischer Hochschulverlag GmbH & Co. KG, Fahrenheitstr. 1, 28359 Bremen. Alle Rechte beim Verlag und bei den jeweiligen Lizenzgebern.

www.maritimepress.de | office@maritimepress.de

Bei diesem Titel handelt es sich um den Nachdruck eines historischen, lange vergriffenen Buches. Da elektronische Druckvorlagen für diese Titel nicht existieren, musste auf alte Vorlagen zurückgegriffen werden. Hieraus zwangsläufig resultierende Qualitätsverluste bitten wir zu entschuldigen.

THE SEA WEST OF SPITSBERGEN

THE OCEANOGRAPHIC OBSERVATIONS OF THE ISACHSEN SPITSBERGEN EXPEDITION IN 1910

BY

BJØRN HELLAND-HANSEN AND FRIDTJOF NANSEN

WITH 6 PLATES

(VIDENSKAPSSELSKAPETS SKRIFTER. I. MAT.-NATURV. KLASSE 1912. No. 12)

UTGIT FOR FRIDTJOF NANSENS FOND

CHRISTIANIA
IN COMMISSION AT JACOB DYBWAD
1912

CONTENTS

	Page
Introduction	1
The Spitsbergen Atlantic Current	13
The Salinity of the Spitsbergen Atlantic Current	14
Seasonal Variations in the Salinity	18
Annual Variations in the Salinity	19
The Temperature of the Spitsbergen Atlantic Current	22
Annual Variations in the Temperature of the Spitsbergen Atlantic Current	27
The "Waves" of the Equilines of the Sections	40
The Branches of the Spitsbergen Atlantic Current	48
The Westward Branch	49
The Northward Branch	50
The Bottom Water	51
The Ice Fjord	54
Literature	65
Table I (Observations at the Stations)	66
Table II (Surface-Observations)	85

Introduction.

Captain GUNNAR ISACHSEN had planned to make oceanographical investigations during his expedition with H. M. S. "Farm" to Spitsbergen in 1909. Unfortunately they had to be given up, as the thermometers ordered from Richter did not arrive until the expedition had left Tromsø and was beyond means of communication. During the second expedition, in 1910, a great many vertical series of deep-sea observations were taken in the waters west of Spitsbergen; and observations of the sea-surface were taken during the whole cruise. The results of these investigations are given in this paper.

Fig. 1 shows the positions of the stations and the dates when these stations were taken. The lines connecting the stations indicate the sections drawn in Pls. IV to VI. It will be seen that the stations were often quite near each other, thus rendering the material very valuable for a close study of many details. Most of the observations have been made by Commanders A. HERMANSEN and J. C. PETERSEN-HANSEN, of the Royal Norwegian Navy. They have taken a very keen interest in the investigations, and have worked almost incessantly as often as they got the opportunity of making oceanographical observations.

The expedition had three water-bottles, *viz.* an Ekman Reversing Water-Bottle, a Pettersson Insulated Water-Bottle of the old model, and a Pettersson-Nansen Water-Bottle (the smaller size). The reversing water-bottle was used in the deep strata from 600 metres downwards, and often also at 400 and 500 metres. It did not always close properly, so that some of the watersamples are of no value on account of admixture with water from the upper layers. These cases will be especially noticed in the tables, where a column contains indications of the instrument used. The insulating water-bottles were used everywhere in the upper strata, except at the surface, where the samples were taken with an ordinary bucket, and at a few stations, where Ekman's apparatus was partly employed.

The water-samples were preserved in bottles with patent lever stoppers of the kind now generally used in oceanographical work; the bottles contained about 250 c.cm. The salinity has been determined by Mohr's

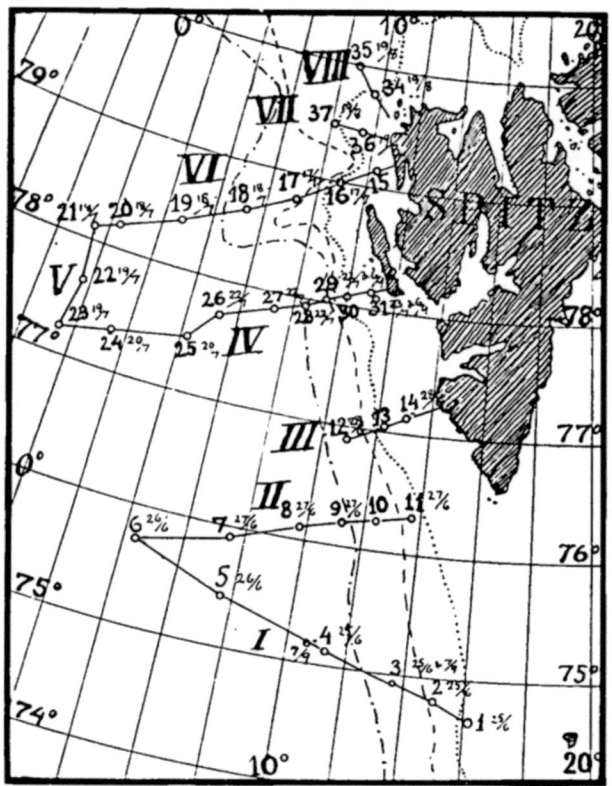

Fig. 1. The oceanographic Stations and Sections of the Isachsen Spitsbergen Expedition 1910. Sect. IX (with Stats. 38—40) north of Spitsbergen should be added.

ordinary chlorine-titration; the titrations were made by Mr. ILLIT GRONDAHL in January and February, 1911. He had standard water from the International Bureau in Copenhagen, and had the silver-solution controlled for every 10th to 15th titration of the water-samples.

The expedition was equipped with two Richter reversing thermometers, two Nansen-thermometers for the insulating water-bottles, and two surface-thermometers.

One of the reversing thermometers was useless, as it did not break off properly. The other one, no. 60, was better, but not quite trustworthy. Thus it happened in some cases that the thermometer evidently gave very erroneous results, *e. g.* at Stat. 2, 600 m. (reading — 3.12° C.), Stat. 7, 600 m. (— 2.92° C.), and several readings at Stat. 32 (readings below — 3° C., or even below — 4° C.). The temperatures found at Stat. 37, between 400 and 800 metres, are also wrong; they correspond closely to the temperature of the air, and it seems probable, that the mercury broken off in the air had not run down again and joined the bulk of the mercury when the water-bottle was sent down. The temperatures of Stat. 34, between 200 and 400, are evidently also wrong for some similar reason, though the temperature of the air was then too low to explain it. But generally the observations made by means of this reversing thermometer seem to be correct; it can to some extent be controlled as far as the "bottom-water" of the Norwegian Sea is concerned. The temperatures observed at a number of stations are demonstrated in Figs. 2—10; a cross indicates that the temperature has been determined by means of the Richter reversing thermometer, while a black dot on the curves indicates the use of an insulated water-bottle with a Nansen-thermometer. It is a striking fact that the differences between temperatures taken with the reversing thermometer at the same levels decrease rapidly with increasing depths, and in depths greater than 1200 metres they very nearly coincide, even though the stations may be far apart. 13 determinations of temperature have been made at a depth of 1200 metres, and give values between — 0.75° and — 1.14°; 9 observations at 1500 metres gave — 0.92° C. and — 1.14° C. as the extreme values. The tables record 7 observations from 2000 metres, all of them ranging between — 1.15° C. and — 1.28° C. — a difference of 0.13° only. This proves that the reversing thermometer has generally worked satisfactorily.

The zero-correction of therm. No. 60 was found to be + 0.047 (19th July, 1909), when the thermometer was quite new from the manufacturer; another determination gave a correction of — 0.004, on the 23rd March, 1911, when the secular depression of zero had probably stopped, and the correction has probably not been much greater during the expedition. The instrumental error of this thermometer has therefore been disregarded in the tables. The corrections due to the secondary temperature-variation of the broken-off mercury have been applied in the general way, by means of the formula $k = \dfrac{(n + T)(T - t)}{6300}$, n being 79, T the reading of the reversing thermometer, and t the indication of the auxiliary thermometer. The reversing thermometer was only used in combination with the Ekman water-bottle.

Only one of the two Nansen-thermometers was employed, *viz*. No. 952 (from C. Richter, Berlin). When tested at the "Physikalisch-Technische Reichsanstalt" of Charlottenburg on January 13, 1910 (where it received the number PTR 37 344), the following corrections were found:

$$\begin{array}{ccccc} \text{at} & 0^0 & 4^0 & 8^0 & 12^0 \text{ C.} \\ k & -0.02^0 & -0.02^0 & -0.01^0 & +0.01 \end{array}$$

Fig. 2. Vertical Temperature-Curves. The readings of the Nansen-thermometer (marked with dots) have not been corrected.

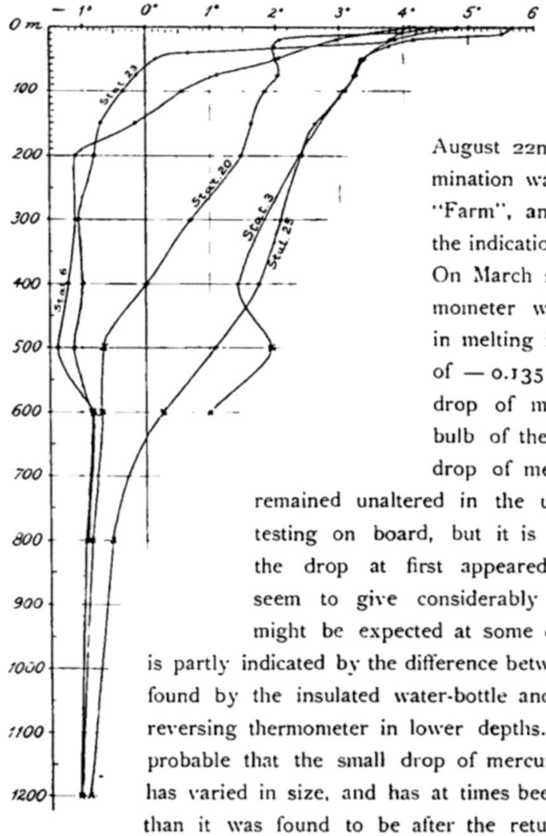

Another determination of zero on April 30th, 1910, gave the same correction at 0^0 ($k = -0.02^0$ C.). On August 22nd, 1910, a zero-determination was made on board the "Farm", and it was found that the indication was 0.12^0 too low. On March 23rd, 1911, the thermometer was examined again; in melting ice it gave a reading of -0.135^0 C., due to a small drop of mercury in the upper bulb of the thermometer. This drop of mercury had evidently remained unaltered in the upper bulb since the testing on board, but it is difficult to tell when the drop at first appeared. The observations seem to give considerably lower values than might be expected at some of the stations; this is partly indicated by the difference between the temperatures found by the insulated water-bottle and those found by the reversing thermometer in lower depths. It is therefore very probable that the small drop of mercury in the upper bulb has varied in size, and has at times been considerably larger than it was found to be after the return of the expedition. This has probably been the case during the first period of the expedition, at Stats. 1—14 in June, 1910 (Sections I, II, and III).

Fig. 2 shows the vertical temperature-curves of Stats. 3 and 6 (Section I), of Stats. 23 and 25 (Section IV), and of Stat. 20 (Section VI, cfr. the chart, Fig. 1). The curves of the two stations of Section I

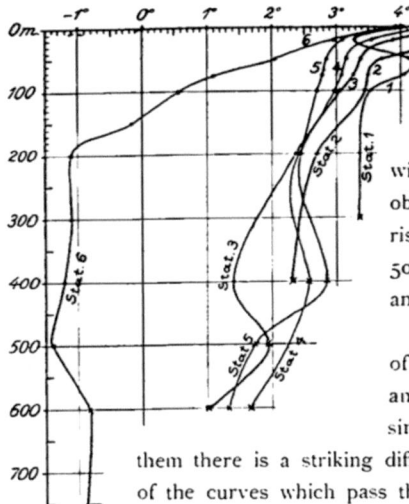

Fig. 3. Vertical Temperature-Curves of Sect. I. Readings of Nansen-thermometer are not corrected.

(Stats. 3 and 6) make a curious bend between the marks representing the lowermost determination with the Nansen-thermometer and the uppermost observation with the reversing thermometer, the observations indicating a considerable rise of temperature between 400 and 500 metres (Stat. 3) or between 500 and 600 metres (Stat. 6).

The vertical temperature-curves of other stations of Section I (Fig. 3) and of Section II (Fig. 4) exhibit similar irregularities. In nearly all of them there is a striking difference between the upper parts of the curves which pass through the observations made with the Nansen-thermometer (marked with dots) and the lower parts passing through the observations of the reversing thermometer (marked with crosses). The rise of temperature occurs at different depths of 300, 400, 500 or even 600 metres, always where the observations of the reversing thermometer begin.

There are obviously errors of some kind in these series of observations, for with the salinities found, the temperature-readings of the Nansen-thermometer would make the densities — at 150 metres at Stat. 13, at 200 m. at Stats. 4 and 5, at 300 m. at Stats. 10 and 11, at 400 m. at Stats. 3 and 8, and at 500 m. at Stat. 6 — appreciably higher than those of the underlying strata, whose temperature was determined by the reversing thermometer. Either the temperature-readings of the reversing thermometer must have been too high, or those of the Nansen-thermometer must have been too low.

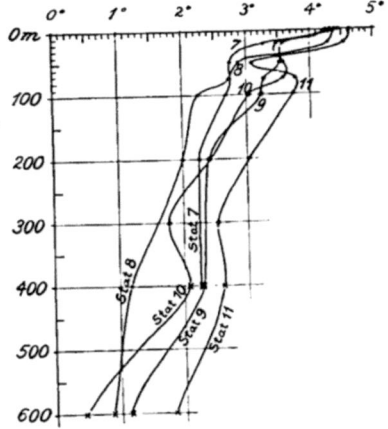

Fig. 4. Vertical Temperature-Curves of Sect. II. Readings of Nansen-thermometer are not corrected.

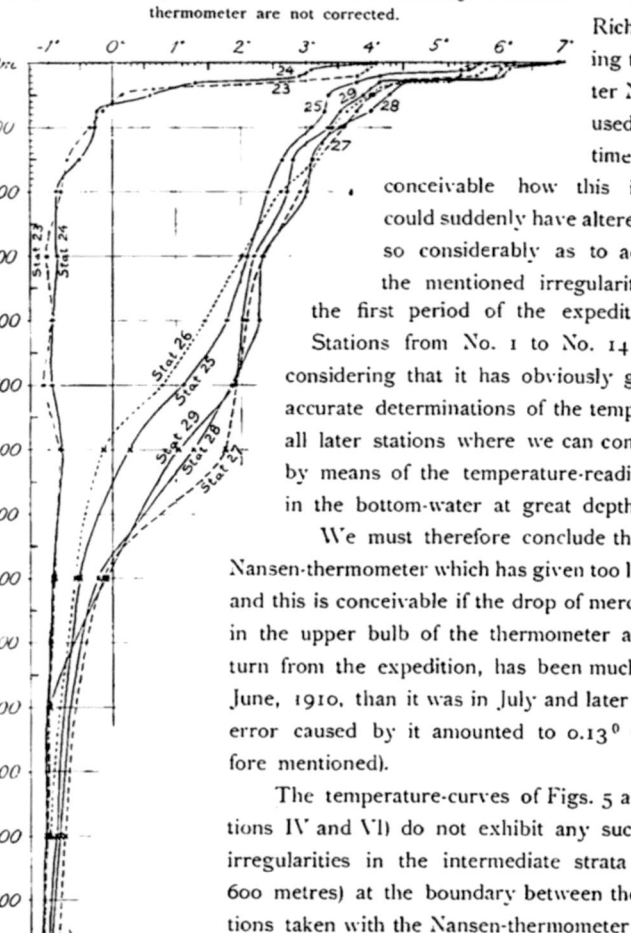

Fig. 5. Vertical Temperature-Curves of Sect. IV. Readings of Nansen-thermometer are not corrected.

The same Richter reversing thermometer No. 60 was used the whole time. It is not conceivable how this instrument could suddenly have altered its error so considerably as to account for the mentioned irregularites during the first period of the expedition (at all Stations from No. 1 to No. 14 in June), considering that it has obviously given very accurate determinations of the temperature at all later stations where we can control them, by means of the temperature-readings taken in the bottom-water at great depths.

We must therefore conclude that it is the Nansen-thermometer which has given too low values, and this is conceivable if the drop of mercury found in the upper bulb of the thermometer after its return from the expedition, has been much larger in June, 1910, than it was in July and later (when the error caused by it amounted to 0.13^0 C., as before mentioned).

The temperature-curves of Figs. 5 and 6 (Sections IV and VI) do not exhibit any such striking irregularities in the intermediate strata (500 and 600 metres) at the boundary between the observations taken with the Nansen-thermometer and those taken with the reversing thermometer. The slight indications of a similar irregularity, which are noticeable, may be accounted for by the error of 0.13^0 C. which the Nansen-thermometer had later. The readings have naturally also to be corrected for the error caused by the adiabatic cooling during the hauling up of the insulated water-bottle; but it does not amount to much in these observations, 0.03^0 C. at most [cf. V. W. Ekman, 1905, p. 16].

On the homeward voyage in September, Captain Isachsen had the observations at some of the former stations repeated. Fig. 7 shows the

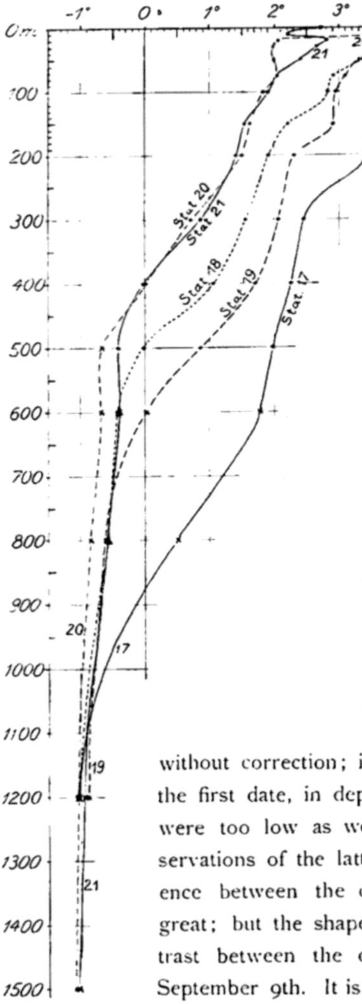

Fig. 6. Vertical Temperature-Curves of Sect. VI. Readings of Nansen-thermometer are not corrected.

temperature-observations at Stat. 3 on June 25th and September 7th; the increase of temperature

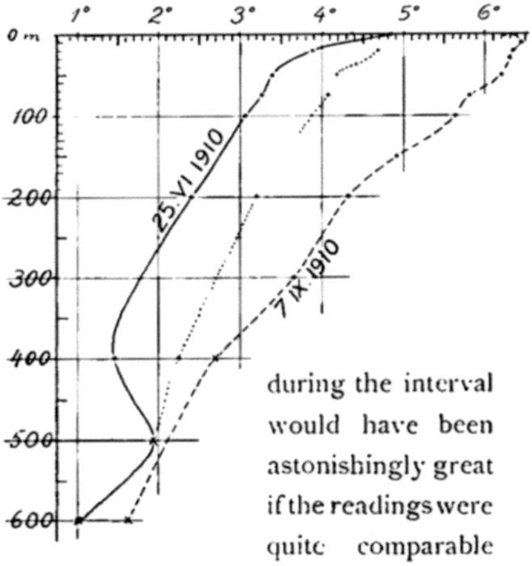

Fig. 7. Vertical Temperature-Curves of June and September 1910, for Stat. 3. Readings of Nansen-thermometer are not corrected in broken and unbroken lines. The dotted line gives the corrected temperatures of June.

during the interval would have been astonishingly great if the readings were quite comparable without correction; it is more probable that the readings of the first date, in depths between the surface and 400 metres, were too low as we have suggested above, while the observations of the latter date were fairly correct. The difference between the curves of Fig. 8, for Stat. 4, is not so great; but the shape of the curves indicates a similar contrast between the observations of June 25th and those of September 9th. It is a striking fact that at both stations the observations taken with the reversing thermometer in June agree very well with those of September, while there is such a great difference between all observations taken with the Nansen-thermometer in the two months. Figs. 9 and 10 — representing the temperature-observations at Stats. 29 and 30 on July 22nd and September 6th give a more probable illustration of the variations between these dates. It is thus probable that the temperature-readings of the Nansen-thermometer have been much too low during the

Fig. 8. Vertical Temperature-Curves of June and September, 1910, for Stat. 4. Readings of Nansen-thermometer are not corrected in broken and unbroken lines. The dotted line gives the corrected temperature of June.

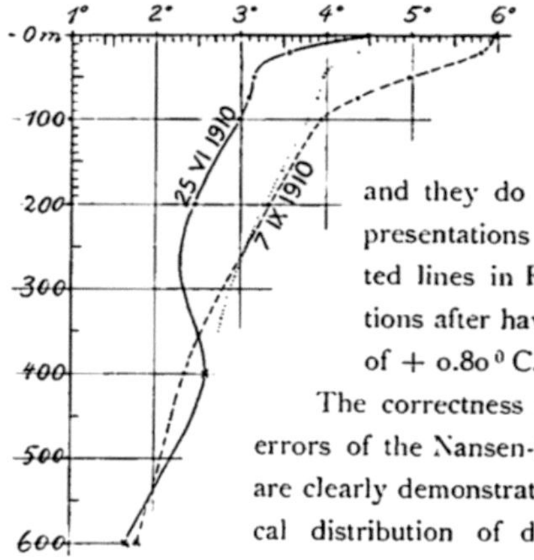

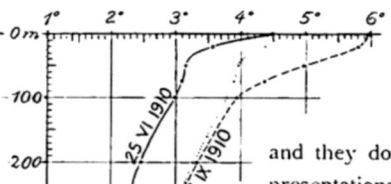

Fig. 9. Vertical Temperature-Curves of July and September, 1910, for Stat. 29.

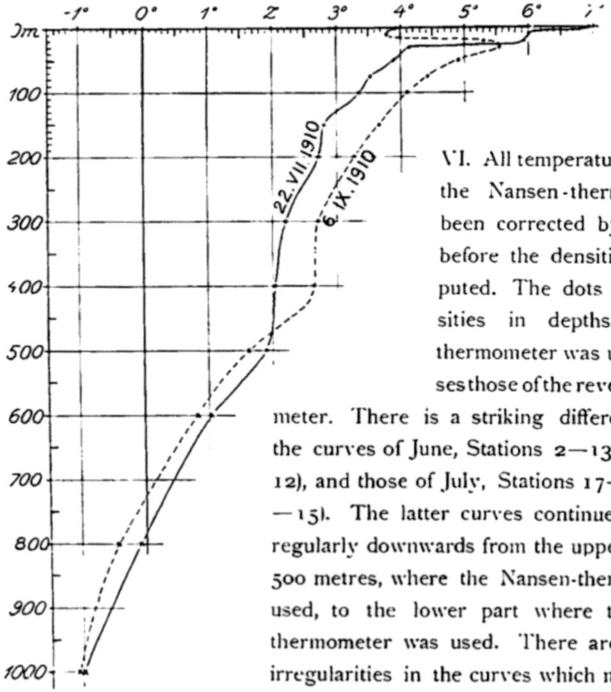

first part of the expedition, in June (Sections I, II, and III), while those of July and later have been about 0.13° C. too low. The curves of Figs. 2—10 represent the temperature-readings of the Nansen-thermometer as they are, without being corrected for these probable errors, and they do not therefore give satisfactory representations of the actual conditions. The dotted lines in Figs. 7 and 8 represent the observations after having been corrected by a correction of + 0.80° C.

The correctness of the above conclusions as to the errors of the Nansen-thermometer during the expedition, are clearly demonstrated by the curves showing the vertical distribution of density at the various stations. In Figs. 11—15 curves are drawn for a great many stations of Sections I to VI. All temperature-readings of the Nansen-thermometer had been corrected by + 0.13° C. before the densities were computed. The dots mark the densities in depths where this thermometer was used, the crosses those of the reversing thermometer. There is a striking difference between the curves of June, Stations 2—13 (Figs. 11 and 12), and those of July, Stations 17—28 (Figs. 13—15). The latter curves continue their course regularly downwards from the upper part, above 500 metres, where the Nansen-thermometer was used, to the lower part where the reversing thermometer was used. There are many small irregularities in the curves which may chiefly be

Fig. 10 Temperature-Curves of July and September, 1910, for Stat. 30.

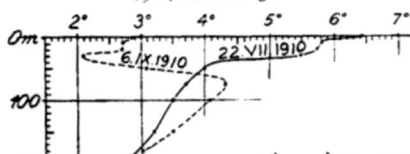

Fig. 11. Curves of Density (σ_t) for Stats. 5—9.

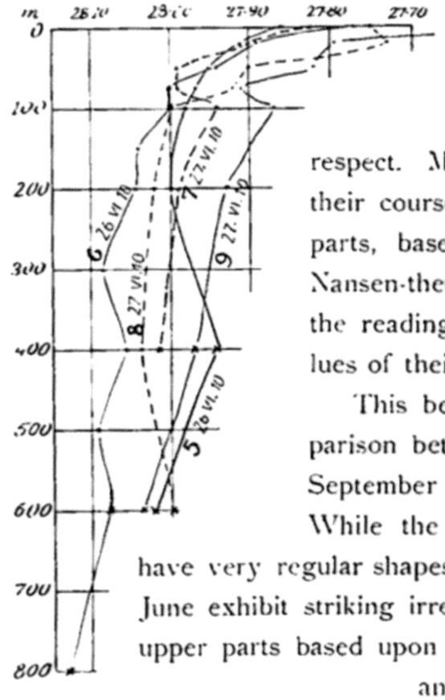

Fig. 12. Curves of Density (σ_t) for Stats. 10—13.

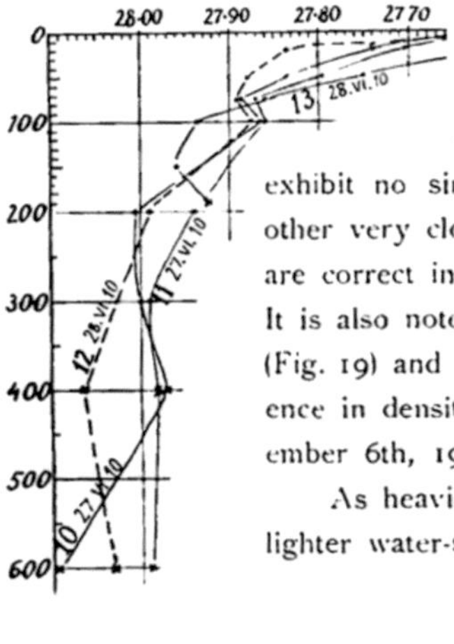

due to inaccuracies of the salinities; but not more in the mentioned depths, between 500 and 600 metres, than in other depths, and the irregularities go in different directions. This proves that there cannot have been any essential difference as to accuracy, between the temperatures taken with the Nansen-thermometer and those of the reversing thermometer.

The curves of density of June (Figs. 11 and 12) are entirely different in this respect. Most of them exhibit a sudden break in their courses at the boundary between their upper parts, based on the temperature-readings of the Nansen-thermometer, and the lower parts based on the readings of the reversing thermometer, the values of their upper parts being obviously too great.

This becomes still more conspicuous by a comparison between the curves of density of June and September at Stations 3 and 4 (Figs. 16 and 17). While the curves of September of both stations have very regular shapes along their whole length, the curves of June exhibit striking irregularities at the boundary between the upper parts based upon the readings of the Nansen-thermometer, and the lower parts based upon the readings of the reversing thermometer. The upper parts of the curves indicate evidently much too high values of density because the temperatures are too low. The curves of July and September for Stat. 29 (Fig. 18) exhibit no similar irregularities, and they follow each other very closely; evidently because the temperatures are correct in their upper as well as their lower parts. It is also noteworthy that the density curves for Stat. 30 (Fig. 19) and for Stat. 31 (Fig. 20) show no great difference in density between July (22nd and 23rd) and September 6th, 1910.

As heavier water-strata cannot as a rule rest upon lighter water-strata, it is fairly easy to see how much

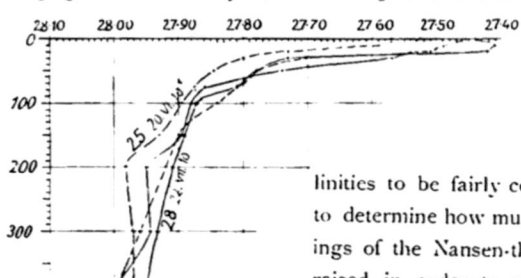

Fig. 13. Curves of Density (σ_t) for Stats. 25—28 (Sect. IV).

the densities of the upper parts of the curves of June have to be reduced in order to give the curves probable shapes. Taking the salinities to be fairly correct, it is then possible to determine how much the temperature-readings of the Nansen-thermometer have to be raised in order to give the probable densities thus found.

The observations of the temperatures of the sea-surface were made with a special thermometer which was immersed in the water taken from the sea-surface with an ordinary bucket. Provided that these observations have been fairly correct and that the salinities found are trustworthy, the densities of the surface-water give a limit below which the densities of the underlying strata may not be reduced by the raising of the temperatures taken with the Nansen-thermometer, not considering small irregularities that may arise from inaccuracies of the observations, and also from the movements of the ship and the water, as the surface-observations being not always taken exactly on the same spot or in the same hour as the observations of the water at 20 metres.

In this manner the surface-observations afford a possibility of finding a probable upper limit of the correction of the readings of the Nansen-thermometer in June, 1910, while the observations with the reversing thermometer, combined with the salinities, give the lower limit of the same correction. By taking the means of the values thus found at each station, we have come to the conclusion that the readings of the Nansen-thermometer should be corrected by about $+ 0.80^0$ C. at all stations of June 25th to 28th (*i. e.* Stats. 1—14). When the readings have been thus corrected we obtain very probable values both of temperature and density.

That the vertical temperature-curves thus obtained have very

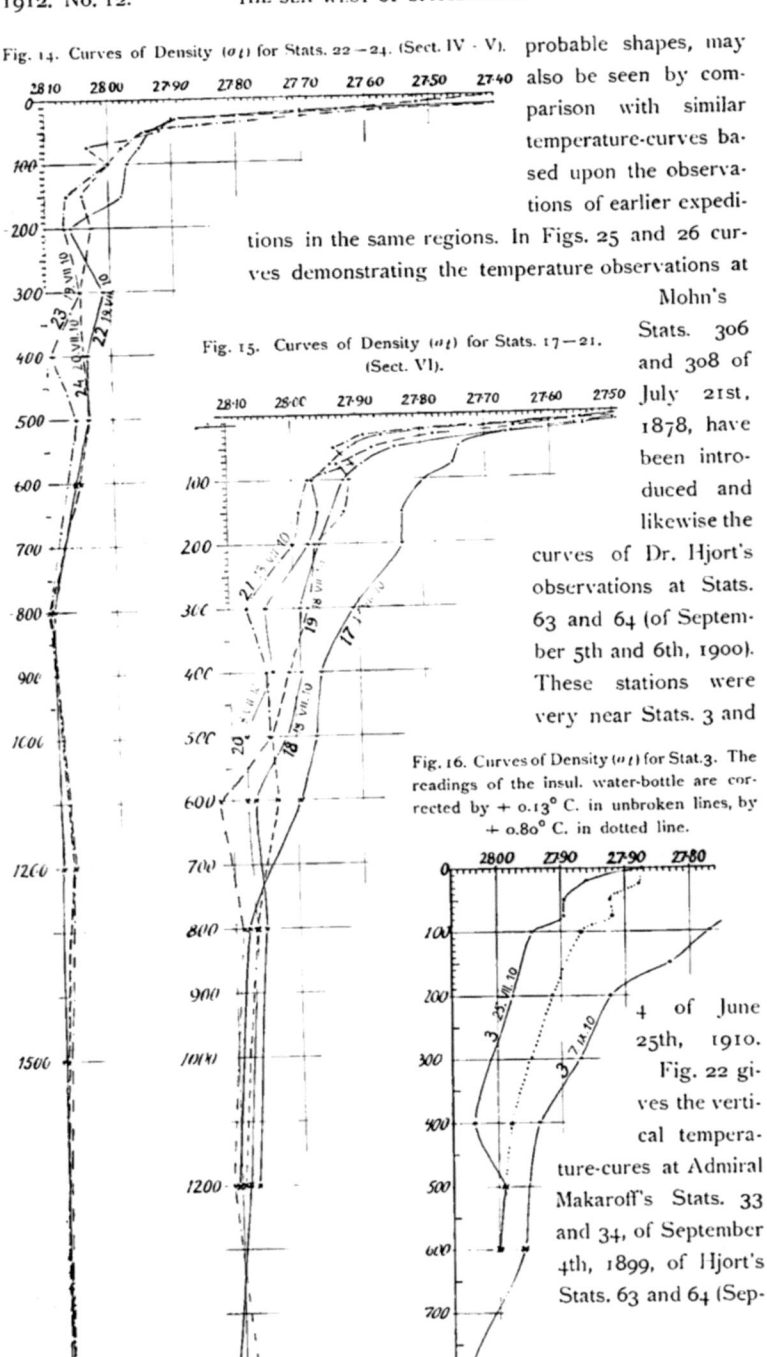

Fig. 14. Curves of Density (σ_t) for Stats. 22—24. (Sect. IV · V).

Fig. 15. Curves of Density (σ_t) for Stats. 17—21. (Sect. VI).

Fig. 16. Curves of Density (σ_t) for Stat. 3. The readings of the insul. water-bottle are corrected by + 0.13° C. in unbroken lines, by + 0.80° C. in dotted line.

probable shapes, may also be seen by comparison with similar temperature-curves based upon the observations of earlier expeditions in the same regions. In Figs. 25 and 26 curves demonstrating the temperature observations at Mohn's Stats. 306 and 308 of July 21st, 1878, have been introduced and likewise the curves of Dr. Hjort's observations at Stats. 63 and 64 (of September 5th and 6th, 1900). These stations were very near Stats. 3 and 4 of June 25th, 1910. Fig. 22 gives the vertical temperature-cures at Admiral Makaroff's Stats. 33 and 34, of September 4th, 1899, of Hjort's Stats. 63 and 64 (Sep-

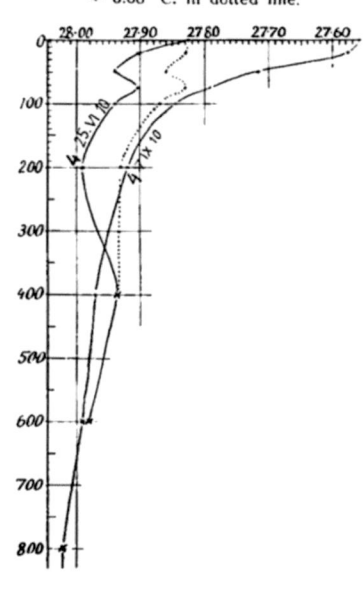

Fig. 17. Curves of Density (σ_t) for Stat. 4. The readings of the Nansen-thermometer are corrected by −0.13° C. in unbroken lines, by +0.80° C. in dotted line.

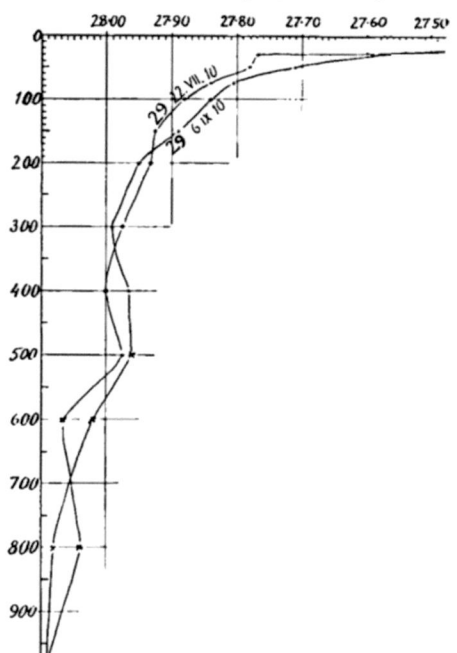

Fig. 18. Curves of Density (σ_t) for Stat. 29.

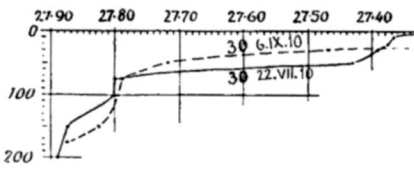

Fig. 19. Curves of Density (σ_t) for Stat. 30.

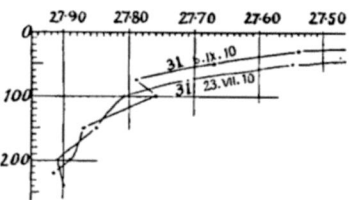

Fig. 20. Curves of Density (σ_t) for Stat. 31.

tember 5th and 6th, 1900) and of Isachsen's Stats. 3 and 4 of September 7th, 1910. All these curves have a striking resemblance to each other in shape, and also to the corrected curves of June 25th, 1910 (see Fig. 25), while the curves based upon the unaltered temperature-readings of the Nansen-thermometer of June 25th, 1910, differ strikingly in their shapes (see Figs. 7 and 8) from all other curves.

The Spitsbergen Atlantic Current.

The oceanographic observations made during the cruise of the Farm in the summer of 1910 are especially valuable for the study of the Spitsbergen Atlantic Current. It was chiefly with this aim in view that the plan of the oceanographic work of the Farm was laid, when Capt. Isachsen discussed it with the writers beforehand. It was thought to be of much interest to have this but little known continuation of the Norwegian Atlantic Current thoroughly investigated.

Our knowledge of the Spitsbergen Atlantic Current had hitherto chiefly been based upon the observations made during the Norwegian North Atlantic Expedition in 1878, when six sections were taken of it in the region between Bear Island and northern Spitsbergen [cf. H. Mohn, 1887]. The temperatures observed during this expedition were remarkably good, considering the imperfection of the instruments of that time; and Mohn's sections give therefore a fairly trustworthy representation of the vertical and horizontal distribution of the temperature in the region of the current. But owing to the imperfect method then generally used in oceanographic researches the values of specific gravity and salinity found were not trustworthy, as might be expected. The description of the vertical and horizontal distribution of the specific gravity in this region, based upon these observations, was therefore more or less misleading.

Since that time observations of importance have been taken in the region of the Spitsbergen Atlantic Current, especially by Prof. SVANTE ARRHENIUS, during the Andrée Expedition in 1896, when a section with six stations (with soundings) was taken westwards from northern Spitsbergen, and by Dr. AXEL HAMBERG during the Nathorst Expedition of 1898, when several stations with deep-sea observations were taken in the region of the Spitsbergen Atlantic Current and its neighbourhood.

Several series of deep-sea observations were also taken in this region by Admiral MAKAROFF in 1899 (his temperatures seem to be trustworthy), by Dr. JOHAN HJORT with the Michael Sars in 1901 and during Prof. G. De Geer's expedition to Spitsbergen in 1908.

During the expedition of the Duke of ORLEANS in the Belgica, in 1905, a most important section with numerous stations of deep-sea soundings was taken in the region north-west of northern Spitsbergen.

Surface-observations have been taken in the sea west of Spitsbergen by a great many expeditions.

Capt. Isachsen's Spitsbergen Expedition of 1910 gives for the first time a series of vertical sections across the Spitsbergen Atlantic Current, by which the vertical and horizontal distribution of the salinity, determined by modern accurate methods, as also the distribution of temperature, can be studied in detail.

Our sections I—VIII (Pls. IV to VI) give therefore a very good representation of the course and extent of this current from the sea northwest of Bear Island, northward along the west coast of Spitsbergen.

The Salinity of the Spitsbergen Atlantic Current.

Our sections demonstrate the decrease in the volume of the Atlantic water with salinities above $35.0\,^0/_{00}$ during its northward course. In Sect. I and II this water has a fairly wide distribution. It is apparently much wider in Sect. I than in Sect. II, but it should be observed that the former section runs obliquely to the direction of the current. In Sect. IV, which runs parallel to Sect. II, the area of the water with salinity above $35.0\,^0/_{00}$ is smaller, and in Sect. VI only a small volume is left; in the latter section there may have been rather more near the continental slope, as in Sect. VII; but in Sect. VIII there are only some few traces of it.

It is evident that during its northward course this Atlantic water is being intermixed with less saline water from the sides. Between the Atlantic water and the Spitsbergen coast in Sect. III there is a considerable volume of water with salinities below $35.0\,^0/_{00}$ and even below $34.9\,^0/_{00}$, and with comparatively low temperatures. This is evidently coast water and to a great extent polar water which has come from the east round South Cape of Spitsbergen with the Spitsbergen Polar Current. This water is probably being gradually intermixed with the Atlantic water on its way northwards along the coast. The effect of this intermixture may perhaps be traced in the Sections III, IV, and VI, the volume of water with salinity less than $34.9\,^0/_{00}$ gradually decreasing northwards, while the volume of the water with salinity between 35.0 and $34.9\,^0/_{00}$ is on the whole increasing.

A similar intermixture with less saline water also takes place on the outer side of the Atlantic Current, and on its under side with the underlying colder water. The precipitation during the whole year naturally produces an appreciable reduction of the salinity of the sea-water in this region where the evaporation from the surface is so small. The vertical circulation created by the cooling of the sea-surface during the winter, helps the vertical intermixture of the strata to a great extent. The melting of ice during the summer naturally lowers the salinity of the surface-layers very much, while the formation of ice during the winter has the opposite effect; but as more ice is probably melted in the region of the Spitsbergen Atlantic Current than is formed there, this process has also a tendency to lower the salinity of its waters, down to certain depths limited by the vertical circulation.

The differences in the area, in the sections, of the Atlantic water with salinities above $35.0^0/_{00}$, are not merely due to the differences in the volume of this water caused by the intermixture of the waters.

A comparison between the isopycnals of Sect. IV and those of Section II shows that the velocity of the Atlantic current was probably greater in the former than in the latter, the isopycnals having a steeper inclination towards the continental slope. We may therefore conclude that the Atlantic Current was narrower in Sect. IV, but had a greater velocity, than in the sections further south. In Sect. VI the velocity of the current was slower in the direction transverse to the section, but the water with salinity above $34.9^0/_{00}$ had a much wider distribution than in Sect. IV.

Our maps for 50 to 400 metres (Pls. II and III) probably give the explanation. The Atlantic Current sends off its westward branch towards Greenland in this region [cf. our description of it, 1909, pp. 280 et seq., Fig. 93, pp. 316 et seq.], and the waters have therefore probably moved in directions more or less oblique to that of the section.

The sections of the Isachsen Expedition may afford a possibility of estimating the rate of the gradual decrease in salinity during the northward flow of the water conveyed by the Spitsbergen Atlantic Current. The results of such an estimate would naturally be of doubtful value, if the salinity of the current can vary much in the same region from year to year. We think, however, that there is no probability of any great annual variations in the salinity of the Spitsbergen Atlantic Current, considering that we have not been able to find such great annual variations in the salinity of the Norwegian Atlantic Current, during the six years 1900 to 1905, from which we have sufficient observations. During this period six vertical sections were taken of the Atlantic Current in the region west of Lofoten and Vesterålen [see our memoir, 1909, Pl. II, etc.]. The maximum salinities in all of them were between 35.21 and $35.25^0/_{00}$; and these high salinities were only found in some small isolated patches in each vertical section, while otherwise the highest salinities were between 35.16 and $35.18^0/_{00}$ in all sections [1]. The current off Lofoten had the highest salinities in May, 1904.

[1] The only exception was the section of February, 1903, where the maximum salinity was $35.15^0/_{00}$; this section was off Vesterålen, and some distance north of the Lofoten sections.

During the spring, summer and autumn of the years 1901 to 1905, eight sections were made across the Norwegian Atlantic Current in the region west-north-west of the Sogne Fjord. The maximum salinities of all these sections vary between $35.31\,^0/_{00}$ and $35.37\,^0/_{00}$. The highest salinities were observed in August and November, 1903, which seems to agree well with the fact that the highest salinities of the Lofoten-sections were found in the following spring (May, 1904). But the difference in salinity between these maximum years and the others is very small in both regions.

The many sections across the Færoe-Shetland Channel taken by the Scotch oceanographers and others during the years from 1902 to 1910 prove that the annual variations in the salinity of the Atlantic water are also as a rule very small in this region where the Atlantic Current flows into the Norwegian Sea, the salinity of the most saline water being most frequently between 35.35 and $35.40\,^0/_{00}$.

We consequently find that the salinity of the waters carried by the Atlantic Current through the Norwegian Sea remains very nearly the same from one year to another, in every region where trustworthy investigations have been carried on; and the salinity decreases gradually during the northward course of the water. We can see no reason why it should be otherwise in its northern continuation called the Spitsbergen Atlantic Current. The probability is therefore that the variations in the salinity of the latter are very small.

In September, 1900, Dr. JOHAN HJORT took a vertical section, (Pl. VI, Sect. H) with three stations (Stats. H. 62—H. 64, Fig. 21), across the eastern part of the Atlantic Current west of the Bear Island Platform [see HELLAND-HANSEN and NANSEN, 1909, Pl. XIV A, Fig. 4]. This section was situated less than one degree of latitude south of the eastern part of Section I (Stats. 1—4). There is a great similarity between the two sections. In the section of 1900 the isohaline of $35.0\,^0/_{00}$ is in about 500 metres near the continental slope at Stat. 63[1], and rises to about 450 m. at Stat. 64, about 100 kilometres farther seawards from the slope. In Section I of June, 1910, the isohaline of $35.0\,^0/_{00}$ is probably in about 500 metres at Stat. 2 near the continental slope, and rises to about 370 m. 100 kilometres farther seawards between Stats. 3 and 4. The volume of Atlantic water

---

[1] In our section (1909, Pl. XIVA, Fig. 4) we have drawn the isohaline of $35.00\,^0/_{00}$ below 600 metres at this station. This is, however, not correct. The salinity in 600 metres was $34.99\,^0/_{00}$ according to the most accurate determination (with Hydrometer of Total Immersion [see 1909, p. 368]) while the value obtained by titration was $35.00\,^0/_{00}$.

with salinities above 35.00 $^0/_{00}$ has consequently had very nearly the same depth in both sections from two different years, 1900 and 1910.

In the section of September, 1900, there is at all three stations a small volume of Atlantic water with salinities about and above 35.10 $^0/_{00}$ in depths of between 60 and 100 metres. There are no such high salinites in Section I of June, 1910. There are, however, indications of a maximum of about 35.06 $^0/_{00}$ and 35.08 $^0/_{00}$ in about 100 metres at Stats. 2, 3 and 5. There are indications of another maximum of 35.08 and 35.09 $^0/_{00}$ near the surface, *e. g.* at Stats. 2 and 4; but the latter maximum will disappear later in the summer, when the salinities of the surface-layers are always much reduced. This is also proved by the observations at Stats. 3 and 4 on September 9th, 1910; the surface-salinity had then been lowered to 34.97 $^0/_{00}$ at Stat. 4, and to 34.56 $^0/_{00}$ at Stat. 3, while there was a maximum of 35.08 $^0/_{00}$ in about 100 metres (also in 50 and 200 m.) at Stat. 3 and 35.06 $^0/_{00}$ at Stat. 4 (between 50 and 200 m.). There is consequently a great similarity also in this respect between Hjort's section of September, 1900, and Isachsen's Section I of June and September, 1910.

We found that the maximum salinity of the waters of the Atlantic Current had decreased on their northward way from about 35.31—35.37 $^0/_{00}$ in the Sognefjord-section, to about 35.21—35.25 $^0/_{00}$ in the Lofoten-section, *i. e.* a decrease of 0.11 $^0/_{00}$. The maximum salinity of Hjort's section westward from Bear Island, of Sept., 1900, was 35.12—35.15 $^0/_{00}$. This is a decrease of 0.10 $^0/_{00}$ from the Lofoten-section. The maximum salinities of Isachsen's sections I, II and III are 35.06—35.09 $^0/_{00}$. This is a decrease of 0.16 $^0/_{00}$ from the Lofoten-section and 0.06 $^0/_{00}$ from the Bear Island section. The distance between the Sognefjord-section and the Lofoten-section is about 360 nautical miles, between the latter and the Bear Island section 450 miles, and between the Bear Island section and Isachsen's Sect. II about 120 miles. The decrease of salinity would then be in the first case 0.03 $^0/_{00}$ in 100 miles, in the second case 0.02 $^0/_{00}$ in 100 miles, and in the last case about 0.05 $^0/_{00}$ in 100 miles [1].

Isachsen's sections farther north show a similar decrease in the maximum salinity northwards. In his Section IV it was 35.03 $^0/_{00}$, in Section VI 35.04 $^0/_{00}$, in Section VII 35.02 $^0/_{00}$, and in Section VIII it was 35.00 $^0/_{00}$. It is on the whole a gradual decrease northwards, of about 0.08 $^0/_{00}$ be-

---

[1] Hjort's water-samples of the Bear Island section were brought home in small bottles with cork stoppers. It is thus possible that the salinities of these samples may have been slightly increased by evaporation through the stoppers. This cannot have been the case to the same extent with Isachsen's water-samples, carried in bottles with patent lever stoppers. It is therefore probable that the above difference between the salinities of Hjort's and Isachsen's sections, is a little too great.

tween his Section II and his Section VIII. The distance between them being about 230 nautical miles, the decrease is about $0.035\,^0/_{00}$ in 100 miles. It seems probable that in the northern regions, where the Atlantic water is covered by a surface-layer with low salinities and also by ice a great part of the year, the decrease in the salinity of the Atlantic water is comparatively slow, because the much lighter surface-layer (as also the ice) is a hindrance to a deep vertical circulation during the winter, which is otherwise an important factor in the intermixture of the underlying water with the less saline surface-water.

At the Belgica-Station 23 (in 77^0 25′ N. Lat., 4^0 3′ W. Long.) in the westward branch of the Spitsbergen Atlantic Current, there was a maximum salinity of $35.00\,^0/_{00}$ in 100 metres. [Duc D'Orléans, 1907, p. 190]. The distance travelled by this Atlantic water was probably nearly the same between the region of Isachsen's Sect. II and this place, as between his Sections II and VIII. The decrease of the salinity was the same in both cases.

All these observations consequently agree fairly well, and we have thus been able to trace approximately the regular changes in the salinity of the waters of the Spitsbergen Atlantic Current on their way northwards and westwards.

Seasonal Variations in the Salinity.

The observations of June, July, and September, at Stats. 3, 4, 29, 30, and 31, indicate the regular decrease in the salinity of the surface-layers during the summer, which occurs more or less in most parts of the North Atlantic and the Norwegian Sea, and is especially striking in the Arctic regions. This reduction of the salinity is due to several causes. By the heating during the summer and the increased admixture of river-water from land, in the warm season when the snow melts, the coast-waters become much lighter, and will spread much farther seawards than in the winter, when they become heavier by cooling (and in the Arctic regions also by the formation of ice, increasing the salinity). Owing to the deflecting effect of the Earth's rotation, they will therefore, in the winter, be forced nearer to the coasts to the right of the current. In the Arctic regions the waters carried by the Arctic and Polar currents are of the same nature as the coast-waters. The salinity of their surface-layers is much reduced by the melting of the floating ice during the warm season, while their salinity is increased during the cold season by the formation of ice on the surface. These waters will consequently have a tendency to spread over wider areas in the summer and autumn than in the winter and spring.

The precipitation has naturally a considerable reducing effect upon the salinity of the surface-layers in these northern regions, as already mentioned. This reduction becomes less conspicuous in the winter, when the vertical circulation helps to intermix the surface-layers with the underlying strata, a process which goes on far less actively in the summer, when the heating of the sea-surface prevents it.

Annual Variations in the Salinity.

Although there are evidently great variations in the temperature of the Spitsbergen Atlantic Current from one year to another, as will be mentioned later, we have not been able to find any similar variations in the salinity of the current, in those few years, from which there are trustworthy determinations of salinity. It has been already mentioned that the salinities of Isachsen's Section I of June, 1910, bear a great resemblance to those of Hjort's Section westward from Bear Island, of September, 1900. The lower salinities of Isachsen's Section I, may be due to the more northerly situation of the section, and do not indicate any appreciable difference in the salinity of the current in the two years, although the difference in temperature was considerable (see later). If the salinity had varied as the temperature, one might have expected higher salinities in 1910 than in 1900.

In 1901 Dr. Hjort made a cruise with the Michael Sars to Spitsbergen and took the following vertical series of observations:

Station	Date 1901	Hour	N. Lat.	E. Long.	Depth Metres	t^0 C.	$S\ ^0/_{00}$	σ_t
84	July 24	1.30 p.m.	$74^0\ 43'$	$17^0\ 10'$	0	4.5		
					200	2.3	35.00	27.98
85a	"	12 MN.	$75^0\ 12'$	$16^0\ 56'$	280	2.2	34.97	.06
85	25	6.30 a.m.	$75^0\ 12'$	$16^0\ 50'$	0	4.32	.70	.51
					50	3.12	.85	.78
					100	2.6	.90	.92
					150	2.10	[35.14]	[28.10]
					200	2.20	34.95	27.95
92	30	3. a.m.	$77^0\ 19,$	$12^0\ 8'$	0	5.3	34.93	.60
					25	5.46	.95	.60
					50	4.1	.97	.78
					100	4.18	35.06	.83
					200	2.62	.01	.90

The salinities here agree well with the salinities of 1910. Hjort's Stat. 84 was very nearly in the same latitude as Isachsen's Stat. 1, and one degree of Longitude farther east. At the latter station the salinities were 35.00 $^0/_{00}$ in 100 metres, and 35.07 $^0/_{00}$ in 200 metres. At Hjort's station the salinity was 35.00 $^0/_{00}$ in 200 metres. Hjort's Stat. 85 was some distance northeast of Isachsen's Stat. 1, and the salinities (between 100 and 280 metres) do not exceed 34.97 $^0/_{00}$, except at 150 metres where 35.14 $^0/_{00}$ was observed, which is, however, obviously erroneous, as is proved by the density. There has evidently been some evaporation through the cork stopper of the bottle in which this water-sample was brought home.

At these stations near Bear Island, the salinities of 1901 may consequently seem to have been somewhat lower than those of 1910; but this may be explained by the fact that Hjort's stations of 1901 were farther east and nearer the Bear Island Platform than Isachsen's station of 1910. The temperatures at Hjort's station were also considerably lower than at Isachsen's.

Hjort's Stat. 92 was a short distance north of Isachsen's Stat. 13, but the salinities were on the whole much higher, and agree better with the salinities observed at Isachsen's Stat. 11 (and other stations of Sections II and I) farther south. The temperatures at Stat. 92 of 1901, were higher than those of Stats. 12—14 of June, 1910, but somewhat lower than those of Stat. 11. This may indicate that at Stats. 12–14 there has been more admixture of the water of the Spitsbergen Polar Current than at Stat. 92 of 1901, while the agreement between the salinities of Stat. 92 and Stat. 11 (and other stations of Sections II and I) of 1910 proves that there has been very little difference in the salinity of the Atlantic water in the two years.

The salinities at Stat. 1 of the De Geer Expedition, of September 2nd, 1908, may seem to have been somewhat (about 0.05 $^0/_{00}$) higher than at Isachsen's Stats. 28 and 29 to the north[1], while at Hamberg's Stat. L, of July 25th, 1898, farther north [HAMBERG, 1906, p. 37] the salinities of the upper strata may seem to have been much the same as at these stations of Isachsen's; but Hamberg's values of salinity are evidently too high, at least those of the deep strata, as is proved by his salinities of the cold bottom-water. In depths of 1000, 1770, 2000, 2700, 2750, and 3160, where the temperatures were between —0.2° C. or — 0.6° C. (in 1000

[1] It is not stated in the paper of „Svenska Hydrografisk-Biologiska Kommissionen" [1911] how the water-samples were taken, in what kind of bottles they were brought home, and when they were titrated. We do not, therefore, know what the degree of accuracy may be, and how far the possibility of evaporation of the samples has been avoided.

metres) and -1.3^0 C., his salinities vary between 35.00 and 35.08 $^0/_{00}$ (only in one case has he a salinity of 34.94 $^0/_{00}$ in 2000 metres). In these cases the error has evidently varied between 0.08 $^0/_{00}$ and 0.16 $^0/_{00}$, at least. It is therefore hardly possible to compare Hamberg's salinities with those of Isachsen's stations. The salinities of Arrhenius' Stations 3 6 north of Isachsen's Section VI are not sufficiently trustworthy for a comparison.

We think that our above discussion of the variations in the salinity of the Atlantic water of the Norwegian Atlantic Current (in the Lofoten-section, and the Sognefjord-section) proves the improbability of any great annual variations in the salinities of the Spitsbergen Atlantic Current. The views held by the Svenska Hydrografisk-Biologiska Kommissionen [1911] in this respect cannot therefore be correct, as we think is even indicated by the observations of the Swedish expedition of 1908, given in their paper [1911, p. 18]. The temperature of the Spitsbergen Atlantic Current was probably comparatively high that year in about 77^0 44' N. Lat., as will be pointed out later. If the views of the Swedish oceanographers were correct, we might therefore expect unusually high salinities in the current that summer, but the maximum salinity at their only station in the current (see Fig. 21, G 1) was 35.10 $^0/_{00}$ in 100 metres, while the maximum salinity at Isachsen's Stat. 28, some distance to the north, was 35.03 $^0/_{00}$ in July, 1910, when the current was probably somewhat colder[1]. The Swedish oceanographers have evidently not been aware of the great stability of the salinities of the Norwegian Atlantic Current in the region to the south; a stability which is proved by all observations during recent years.

The Swedish oceanographers maintain [1911, p. 7] that the high salinities observed at Arrhenius' Stats. 3—6 are perfectly trustworthy. We think that the vertical series of observations themselves at these stations prove sufficiently that this cannot be the case. By computing the densities from the observed temperatures and salinities one finds absurd values, not to mention that at most stations water with comparatively high density is frequently resting on much lighter water. A few examples may be mentioned.

---

[1] The Swedish Stat. II was near the coast (in 78" 5' N., 12" 50' E.) and within the waters of the Atlantic Current. The salinity of 35.14 $^0/_{00}$ found in 200 metres at this station is erroneous, as is clearly proved by the density of 28.03, the density of the underlying water being 27.89, and that of the overlying 27.86.

Station	Depth	σ_t	Station	Depth	σ_t
Stat. 3 ...	60 m.	27.95	Stat. 4 ...	400 m.	28.20
	80 „	27.68		850 „	28.07
Stat. 3 ...	300 m.	28.03	Stat. 6 ...	500 m.	28.13
	500 „	27.85		850 „	28.06

Such values are impossible, and a density such as 28.20 (Stat. 4, 400 m.) does not exist anywhere in the Ocean, except perhaps in the cold bottom-water in some exceptional localities. If the Swedish oceanographers had been aware of this they would hardly have been able to maintain that salinities between 35.20 and 35.30 $^0/_{00}$ may occur in the Spitsbergen Atlantic Current. We think that the facts mentioned above prove the impossibility of salinities as high as these ever occurring in this Current.

In the vertical sections of the Atlantic Current west of Lofoten, the highest salinities, in all years when the observations were taken, were between 35.21 and 35.25 $^0/_{00}$; and these high values were only observed in small isolated patches in each section, otherwise the highest salinities were between 35.16 and 35.18 $^0/_{00}$. How then would it be possible to expect such high salinities in the current west of Spitsbergen? And if salinities as high as 35.29 $^0/_{00}$ could occur in the Atlantic Current in 79° N. Lat., what would the salinity of this water have been when it passed the region of Lofoten, and how much more when it passed through the Færoe-Shetland Channel? Nansen [1906] has proved that bottom-water with unusually high salinities may be found in the Arctic seas, the high salinity being produced by the formation of ice on the sea-surface. But this is only where the sea is shallow, and the water very cold. There is no such possibility in the warm waters of the Spitsbergen Atlantic Current.

The Temperature of the Spitsbergen Atlantic Current.

By computing the mean temperature in each vertical section of the waters carried by the Spitsbergen Atlantic Current, it might be possible to get some rough estimate of the loss of heat of these waters during their northward course. A calculation such as this presents, however, several difficulties, which will necessarily make the result uncertain.

On the one hand for instance, it is difficult to tell where the limits of the Atlantic water are in each section. One can hardly go by the same salinity, because this decreases gradually northwards, as was mentioned above, the waters carried by the current, having a considerably lower salinity in the region of Sect. VI than in the region of Sect. I and II. If we were to take the decrease in the maximum salinities as an indicator, it might, for instance, be assumed that the decrease in the salinity of the current was about 0.05 $^0/_{00}$ from the region of Section I to that of Sect. VI, considering that the observed maximum salinities have decreased from between 35.06 and 35.09 $^0/_{00}$ to between 35.01 and 35.04 $^0/_{00}$. If, therefore, one took, for instance, the isohaline of 35.0 $^0/_{00}$ as indicating the boundary of the waters carried by the current through Section I, the corresponding boundary-line of Section VI would be the isohaline of 34.95 $^0/_{00}$. To judge from our sections, Pls. IV—VI, this might also seem a reasonable method; but as it would be somewhat complicated, without warranting correspondingly accurate results, and as the boundary-line thus found would at most stations lie approximately in 450 and 500 metres, we consider it to be sufficiently accurate for our purpose simply to take the mean of the temperatures of the water-strata down to 450 or 500 metres at all stations within the current in each section, which means, in Sect. I, Stats. 2 to 5; in Sect. II, Stats. 7—11; in Sect. IV, Stats. 25—29, and in Sect. VI, Stats. 17—19. We have here left out the stations near the coast, where the depths were less than 400 metres. As the temperatures of the surface-layers are very dependent on the radiation of the sun, the temperature of the atmosphere and the melting of ice, etc., they ought to be excluded, and the means should only be taken of the strata between 500 metres and a certain depth below the surface.

Another difficulty is involved in the circumstance that the dates of the sections differ much. It is obvious, for instance, that the mean temperature of Sect. VI, taken on July 17th—18th, 1910, should be comparatively warmer than that of Sect. I which was taken on June 25th—26th, or 22 days earlier in the summer.

The observations repeated in September at Stats. 3, 4, 29, 30, and 31, afford, however, some means of finding out what the rise in the temperature of the water-strata may be during the summer in the same localities. By taking the mean of the temperatures for 50, 150, 250, 350, and 450 metres, we may get a fairly correct value for the mean temperature of the whole volume of water between the surface and 500 metres. The temperatures may easily be taken from vertical temperature-curves (see Figs. 22—30). The following table gives the results for Stats. 3, 4, and 29. The water at Stats. 30 and 31 was too shallow (195 and 235 metres) to give trustworthy results for such a comparison.

Depth	Stat. 3			Stat. 4			Stat. 29		
	25. VI. 10	7. IX. 10	Difference	25. VI. 10	7. IX. 10	Difference	22. VII. 10	9. IX. 10	Difference
	⁰ C.	⁰ C.	⁰ C.	⁰ C.	⁰ C.	⁰ C.	⁰ C.	⁰ C.	⁰ C.
50	4.2	6.33	2.13	3.96	5.1	1.14	3.90	5.04	1.14
150	3.5	5.05	1.55	3.5	3.75	0.25	2.93	3.79	0.86
250	3.0	4.1	1.1	2.9	3.2	0.3	2.58	3.1	0.52
350	2.5	3.25	0.75	2.75	2.7	—0.05	2.25	2.8	0.55
450	2.1	2.4	0.3	2.9	2.3	—0.6	1.97	2.2	0.23
Mean	3.06	4.23	1.17	3.20	3.41	0.21	2.73	3.39	0.66
100	3.87	5.77	1.90	3.79	4.08	0.29	3.48	4.23	0.75
200	3.20	4.46	1.26	3.26	3.46	0.20	2.84	3.40	0.56
300	2.73	3.79	1.06	2.93	2.95	0.02	2.35	2.84	0.49
400	2.25	2.70	0.45	2.59	2.49	—0.10	2.16	2.77	0.61
Mean	3.01	4.18	1.17	3.14	3.25	0.10	2.71	3.31	0.60

But as the surface-layers are on the whole very variable, especially in these regions, where there is so much lighter surface-water, and as their temperatures vary much with the season, it may be advisable to leave them out in our comparison. For the sake of convenience we have therefore chosen the temperatures at 100, 200, 300, and 400 metres. The means of these temperatures may give fairly trustworthy values for the mean temperature of the whole volume of water between 50 and 450 metres of depth. The results are given in the second part of our table. There is, however, no great difference between them and the former ones.

The increase of temperature between June and September was very much greater at Stat. 3 (+ 1.17⁰ C.) than at Stat. 4 (+ 0.21⁰ C.). This proves the necessity of comparing the observations at as many stations as possible in order to get a fairly trustworthy estimate of the rate of the heating of the waters of the current during the summer. The increase of temperature at Stat. 3 was from 3.01⁰ C. on June 25th to 4.18⁰C. on September 7th; i. e. 1.17⁰ C. in 74 days, or about 0.16⁰ C. in 10 days.

If we take the means of Stats. 3 and 4 combined, the increase of temperature would be from 3.08⁰ C. on June 25th, to 3.72⁰ C. on September 7th, i. e. an increase of 0.64⁰ C. in 74 days, or about 0.09⁰ C. in 10 days.

The corresponding increase of temperature was, at Stat. 29, from 2.71⁰ C. on July 22nd, to 3.31⁰ C. on September 6th; i. e. an increase of 0.60⁰ C. in 46 days, or about 0.13⁰ C. in 10 days.

The values thus obtained by comparing some few vertical temperature-curves cannot, however, be considered very accurate, also for this reason, that the conditions in the sea may evidently change much in a short time, as we have previously pointed out; and there are probably great periodical or unperiodical vertical movements of the water-strata, by which a stratum with comparatively low temperatures, may for instance at one time be observed in 500 metres, and at another time in 450 metres or higher. Such a vertical movement may possibly explain why at Stat. 29, the curve of September 6th shows lower temperatures, in depths below 500 metres, than the curve of July 22nd (see Fig. 29). If the water-strata of the September-curve be lowered about 40 metres, the two curves would nearly coincide below the depth of 500 metres, while the difference between them would be somewhat increased above that level.

By taking the mean increase of temperature from June and July to September at the three Stations mentioned, 3, 4 and 29, we find an increase of $0.10°$ C. in 10 days in the mean temperature of the water of the Spitsbergen Atlantic Current between 50 and 450 metres of depth. This value does not give the increase in the temperature of the same water that is continually moving northwards; but it indicates the increase in the temperature in the locality where the water is continually being renewed.

In the vertical sections of the Norwegian Atlantic Current northwestwards from the Sognefjord, we have found [see 1909, p. 230] an increase in the mean temperature of the Atlantic water (except the surface-strata) with salinity above $35.00\ °/_{00}$, from $7.23°$ C. on May 23rd—24th, 1903, to $7.66°$ C. on August 10th, 1903; *i. e.* an increase of $0.43°$ C. in 78 days, or $0.055°$ C. in 10 days.

From August 10th, 1903, to November 17th—18th, 1903, the corresponding increase was from $7.66°$ C. to $8.13°$ C.: *i. e.* $0.47°$ C. in 99 days, or $0.047°$ C. in 10 days.

The increase in the temperature of the water of the Atlantic Current should consequently be much slower in the region of the Sognefjord-sections, or in about $62°$ N. Lat. than in the region of Isachsen's Sects. I and IV, or in about $75°$ and $78°$ N. Lat. The values are not, however, quite comparable, as Isachsen's Stats. 3, 4, and 29, were in the warmest part of the current, *i. e.* near its right side, while the mean temperatures of the Sognefjord-section were the means of all observations in the Atlantic water of the whole section.

The mean temperatures of the water between 50 metres and 450 metres (computed from the temperature at 100, 200, 300, and 400 metres as above) are the following in Isachsen's four sections of the Spitsbergen Atlantic Current:

Section	Stations	Date	Mean t. ⁰C.	Mean t. ⁰ on July 20th
I	2— 5	25—26, VI	3 15⁰ C.	3.40⁰ C.
II	7—11	27 , VI	3.02	3.25
IV	25—29	20—22, VII	2.70	2.70
VI	17—19	17—18, VII	2.50	2.53

As the sections were taken at different dates, their mean temperatures have to be corrected by the probable change in the difference of time. This has been done in the last column, where the temperatures have been corrected to what they would have been on July 20th, if they had increased at the rate of 0.10⁰ C. in 10 days, as found above.

The decrease of the mean temperatures thus obtained are the following:

	Difference in Mean t.⁰C	Mean distance between Sections	Decrease in t.⁰C. in 10 naut. miles
Between Sects. I and II	0.15⁰ C.	64 naut. miles	0.023⁰ C.
„ „ II „ IV	0 55	110 „ „	0.05
„ „ IV „ VI	0.17	56 „ „	0.03
Between Sects. I and VI	0 87⁰ C.	230 naut. miles	0.038⁰ C.

These values cannot be expected to give the real decrease in the temperature of the water on its way northwards from the one section to the other, as the water which was observed, *e. g.* in Section VI in July, 1910, may have had a mean temperature comparatively quite different from that of Sect. I when it passed this same region.

By comparing the mean temperatures of the Atlantic water of the Sognefjord-section, in May of the years 1901—1903, with those of the Atlantic water of the Lofoten-section of the following years, we have found [see 1909, p. 180] an average decrease in the temperature of 1.18⁰ C. The distance between the sections is about 360 nautical miles. The decrease should consequently be about 0.033⁰ C. in 10 naut. miles.

The mean temperature of the Atlantic water of the Lofoten Section, in May of the four years 1901—1904, was 5.42⁰ C. According to the probable rate of the increase of the temperature during the summer, this should correspond to a mean of about 5.55⁰ C. in June. The difference between this value and the mean temperature of the water of the Atlantic Current in Isachsen's Sect. I is 2.40⁰ C. The distance between the sections is about 470 nautical miles, thus showing a decrease of 0.05⁰ C. in 10 naut. miles. This is of course a rough approximation only, as the annual variations could not be considered.

Annual Variations in the Temperature of the Spitsbergen Atlantic Current.

We have found that there are considerable variations in the mean temperature of the Norwegian Atlantic Current [cfr. 1909, p. 171 *et seq.*]. It is, therefore, probable that there are similar variations in the Spitsbergen Atlantic Current which is a continuation of this current. There is unfortunately no great material of observations from previous years which may be used for a study of these annual variations.

Dr. Hjort's section of September 4th—6th, 1900 (Fig. 21, Stat. H 62, H 63, and H 64; cfr. Pl. VI, Sect. II), westward from Bear Island, was taken about 40 nautical miles farther south and 72 days later in the season than Isachsen's Sect. I of June 25th, 1910. It might, therefore be expected that the Atlantic water of the former would be warmer than that of the latter. This is not the case, however. The isotherm of 2^0 C. lies higher in the section of 1900 than the isohaline of $35.0\,^0/_{00}$; in Sect. I of 1910 it lies lower than that isohaline.

The mean temperature of the water between 50 and 450 m. at Stations 2, 3, 4, and 5 of Sect. I was 3.15^0 C.[1]. The mean temperature of the water in the same depths at Hjort's Stats. 63 and 64 was 2.68^0 C. If, in order to make the mean temperature of Section I fully comparable with that of Hjort's section, the former should be corrected for the probable difference in temperature owing to its more northern latitude and the earlier season (according to the values of these differences found above, *viz.* 0.038^0C. for every 10 naut. miles, 0.10^0 C. for every 10 days), we obtain a mean temperature of 4.02^0 C., which is consequently 1.34^0 C. higher than the corresponding mean temperature at Stats. 63 and 64 of 1900. If Isachsen's more northern sections be corrected in the same manner, their mean temperatures of the water between 50 and 450 metres should be: Sect. II (Stats. 7—11) = 4.1^0 C.; Sect. IV (Stats. 25—29) = 3.9^0 C.; Sect. VI (Stats. 17—19) = 4.0^0 C. These values consequently represent the mean temperatures which the volume of Atlantic water of the different sections might have had when they were in the latitude of Hjort's Stats. 63 and 64 (about 74^0 15′ N. Lat.), and if they had been there on September 5th. These values agree very well with each other.

We may thus conclude that in the sea west and northwest of the Bear Island submarine shelf, the waters of the Spitsbergen Atlantic Current were considerably warmer in the summer of 1910 than in the summer of

---

[1] It makes no great difference if Stats. 5 and 2 be left out, the corresponding mean temperature of Stats. 3 and 4 being 3.08^0 C., and of Stats. 2, 3, and 4, 3.14^0 C.

1900. According to the mean temperature of this water in Isachsen's Sect. I, the difference should have been $1.34°$ C.

The vertical series of observations which Dr. Hjort took in the Spitsbergen waters in 1901 (see above, p. 19), give no trustworthy information regarding the temperature of the current in that year, as they are far too few and not deep enough. Hjort's Stat. 92 may, however, give some indication, if we compare the temperatures of the Atlantic water, with salinities above $35.0\,°/_{00}$ (i. e. in 100 and 200 metres) at this station with the corresponding temperatures of the Atlantic water at Isachsen's Stat. 11. The temperature of the Atlantic water was in 100 metres $0.37°$ C., and in 200 metres $1.24°$ C. colder at Stat. 92, of July 30th, 1901, than at Stat. 11, of June 27th, 1910. Owing to the earlier season (33 days earlier) the temperatures of 1910 should be comparatively still warmer; but on the other hand this may be assumed to be approximately counterbalanced by the more southerly situation. It is consequently possible that the Spitsbergen Atlantic Current was somewhat colder in 1901 than in 1910, but how much cannot be determined. If we were to judge from the above temperatures in 100 and 200 metres, the difference between the mean temperatures for 100—400 metres might have been approximately something like $0.6°$ C. But this is naturally very uncertain, as there are far too few observations.

The differences in the temperature of the water in different years where there are no complete vertical sections, may be studied by comparing the vertical temperature-curves of stations that have been taken as nearly as possible in the same locality and at the same time of the year. In our Memoir on "The Norwegian Sea" we have proved that owing to various, probably vertical as well as horizontal, movements of the waters, which are still but little known, there may be great differences between the observations at stations that are quite near each other. It is therefore obvious that for the study of the changes in the temperature of a current, it would be desirable to have for comparison as many vertical temperature-curves as possible from the same region.

Fig. 21 gives the positions of some stations of the Norwegian North-Atlantic Expedition of 1878 (M 283—M 361), the Andrée Expedition of 1896 (A 3—A 10), the Nathorst Expedition of 1898 (L—U), the Makaroff Expedition 1899 (Ma 5—Ma 34), Hjort's Expedition 1900 (H 62—H 65), the Belgica Expedition 1905 (B 3, B 11 a), De Geer's Expedition 1908 (G 1), and Isachsen's Expedition 1910 (1—35).

Fig. 22 gives the vertical temperature-curves of September 7th, 1910, at Isachsen's Stats. 3 and 4, as also those of Hjort's Stats. 63 and 64 (H 63

Fig. 21. Oceanographic Stations: 1—37 of the Isachsen Exp. 1910; M 283 —M 301 of the Norw. N. Atlantic Exp. 1878; A 3—A 10 of the Andrée Exp. 1896; L—U of the Nathorst Exp. 1898; Ma 5—Ma 34 of Makaroff's Exp. 1899; H 62—H 65 of the Michael Sars Exp. 1900; B 3 & B 11 a of the Belgica Exp. 1905; G 1 of the De Geer Expedition 1908.

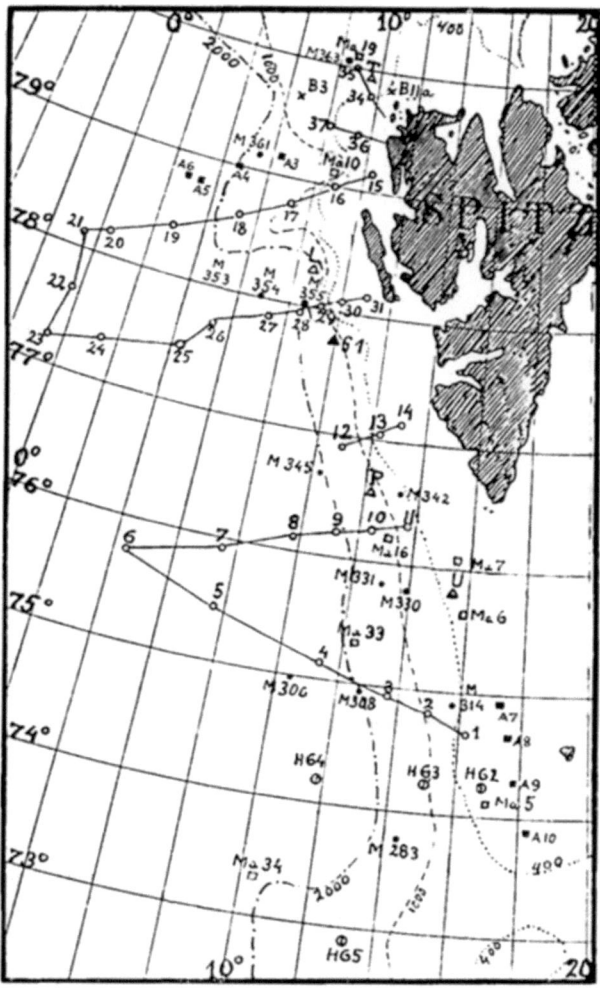

and H 64) of September 5th and 6th, 1910. The latter stations were respectively about 40 and 56 nautical miles south of the former. Their distances west from the continental slope (of the seabottom) were very similar, so that their situation in the northward-flowing current should be approximately the same, Stat. 63 having a somewhat more easterly

Fig. 22.

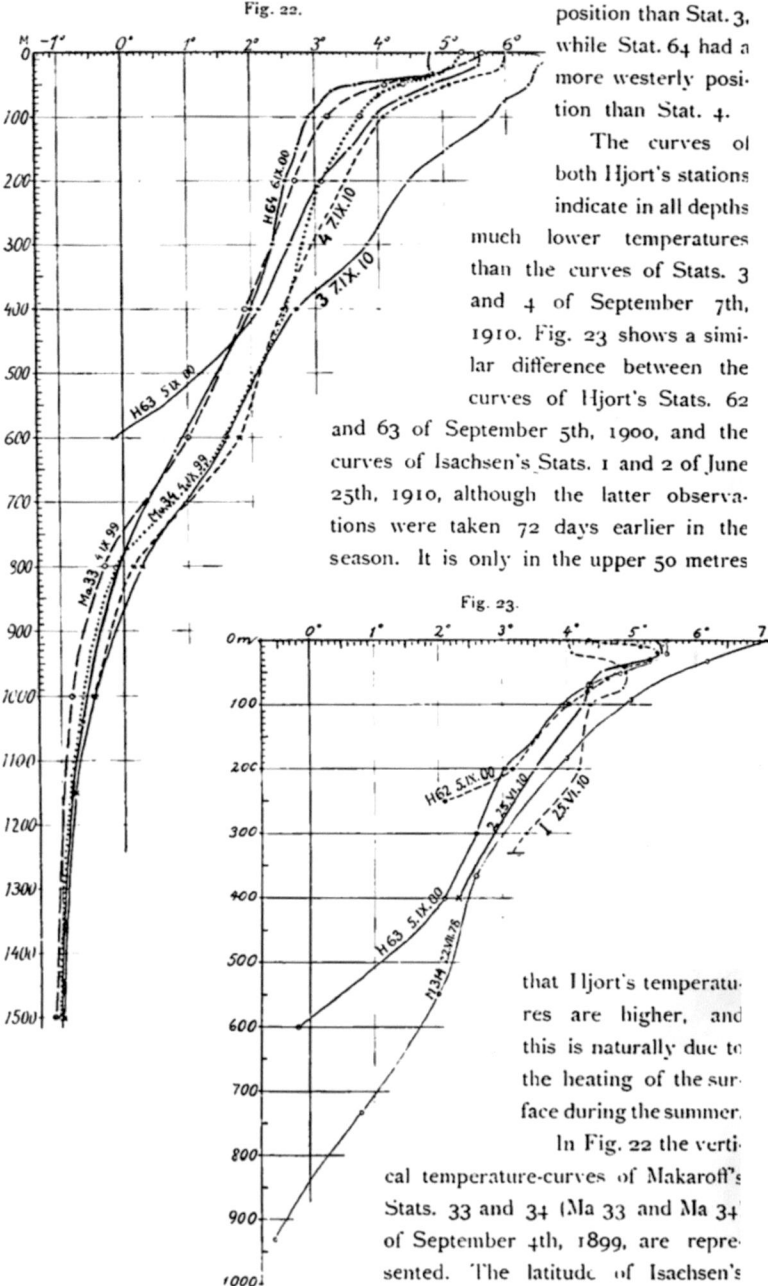

Fig. 23.

position than Stat. 3, while Stat. 64 had a more westerly position than Stat. 4.

The curves of both Hjort's stations indicate in all depths much lower temperatures than the curves of Stats. 3 and 4 of September 7th, 1910. Fig. 23 shows a similar difference between the curves of Hjort's Stats. 62 and 63 of September 5th, 1900, and the curves of Isachsen's Stats. 1 and 2 of June 25th, 1910, although the latter observations were taken 72 days earlier in the season. It is only in the upper 50 metres that Hjort's temperatures are higher, and this is naturally due to the heating of the surface during the summer. In Fig. 22 the vertical temperature-curves of Makaroff's Stats. 33 and 34 (Ma 33 and Ma 34 of September 4th, 1899, are represented. The latitude of Isachsen's

Stats. 3 and 4 was respectively only about 27 and 14 minutes more southerly than Makaroff's Stat. 33, while they were about 1° 33′ and 1° 46′ more northerly than Makaroff's Stat. 34. The meridian of Makaroff's station 33 was be-

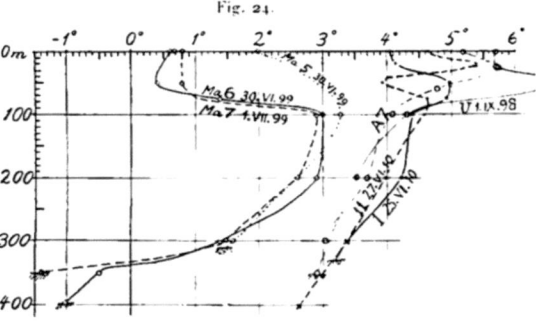

Fig. 24.

tween those of Stats. 3 and 4, and that of his Stat. 34 one degree more westerly than Stat. 4 (see Fig. 21) The observations at all four stations were taken in the first week of September of 1899 and 1910. Both Makaroff's curves show much lower temperatures than those of Stats. 3 and 4, especially in depths of less than 400 metres.

The mean temperature of the water between 50 and 450 metres at Makaroff's two stations was 2.76° C. while the corresponding mean temperature for Stats. 3 and 4 was 3.82° C. If these temperatures were comparable, the Atlantic water should thus have been about 1.06° C. colder in 1899 than in 1910.

The vertical temperature-curves of Makaroff's Stats. 5, 6, and 7 (Fig. 21, Ma 5, Ma 6, and Ma 7) of June 30th and July 1st, 1899, show much lower temperatures than the curves of Isachsen's Stats. 1 and 11 of June 25th and 27th, 1910 (see Fig. 24). All these observations thus point in the same direction. Hjort's Stat. 64 of September, 1900, was about midway between Makaroff's Stats. 33 (about 55 naut. miles to the north-northwest) and 34 (see Fig. 21). The vertical curves of both Makaroff's stations show higher temperatures than the curve of Stat. 64 (see Fig. 22). The following table gives the temperatures in 100, 200, 300 and 400 metres at Makaroff's two stations (Ma 33, Ma 34) and Hjort's station H 64:

Depth in metres	Ma 33 4. IX. 99	Ma 34 4. IX. 99	Mean of Ma 33 & 34	H 64 6. IX. 00
100 m	3.2⁰ C.	3.7⁰ C.	3.45⁰ C.	2.90⁰ C.
200 „	2.7	3.1	2.9	2.51
300 „	2.3	2.8	2.55	2.31
400 „	1.9	2.5	2.2	1.98
Mean	2.52⁰ C.	3.02⁰ C.	2.77⁰ C.	2.43⁰ C.

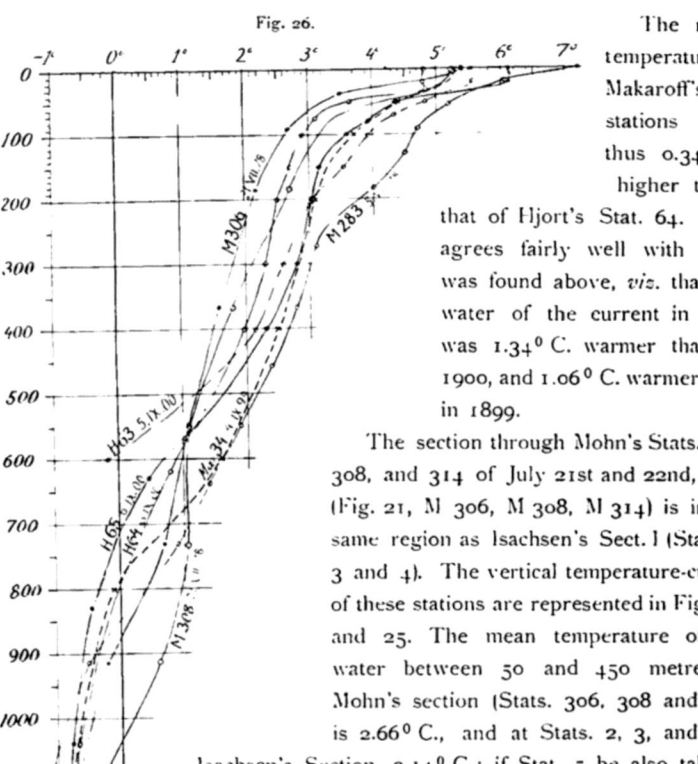

Fig. 26.

The mean temperature of Makaroff's two stations was thus 0.34° C. higher than that of Hjort's Stat. 64. This agrees fairly well with what was found above, *viz.* that the water of the current in 1910 was 1.34° C. warmer than in 1900, and 1.06° C. warmer than in 1899.

The section through Mohn's Stats. 306, 308, and 314 of July 21st and 22nd, 1878 (Fig. 21, M 306, M 308, M 314) is in the same region as Isachsen's Sect. I (Stats. 2, 3 and 4). The vertical temperature-curves of these stations are represented in Figs. 23 and 25. The mean temperature of the water between 50 and 450 metres in Mohn's section (Stats. 306, 308 and 314) is 2.66° C., and at Stats. 2, 3, and 4 of Isachsen's Section, 3.14° C.; if Stat. 5 be also taken it is 3.15° C. As the observations at Isachsen's stations were taken 27 days earlier in the season than those at Mohn's stations, the mean temperature should be increased to 3.41° C. in order to be comparable with that of Mohn's section. The waters of the current should accordingly have been about 0.75° C. colder in 1878 than in 1910, in this region.

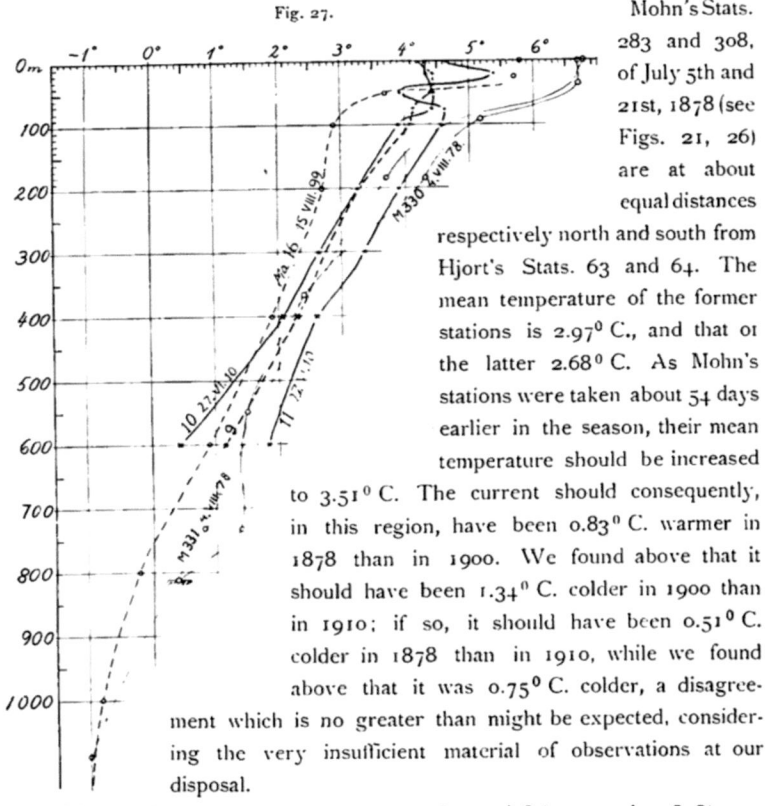

Fig. 27.

Mohn's Stats. 283 and 308, of July 5th and 21st, 1878 (see Figs. 21, 26) are at about equal distances respectively north and south from Hjort's Stats. 63 and 64. The mean temperature of the former stations is 2.97° C., and that of the latter 2.68° C. As Mohn's stations were taken about 34 days earlier in the season, their mean temperature should be increased to 3.51° C. The current should consequently, in this region, have been 0.83° C. warmer in 1878 than in 1900. We found above that it should have been 1.34° C. colder in 1900 than in 1910; if so, it should have been 0.51° C. colder in 1878 than in 1910, while we found above that it was 0.75° C. colder, a disagreement which is no greater than might be expected, considering the very insufficient material of observations at our disposal.

Mohn's Stats. 306, 308, 314, 330 and 331 (of August 4th, 1878), 342 and 345 (of August 6th and 7th, 1878) are between, as well as north and south of Isachsen's Sections I and II (see Fig. 21). The mean temperature of all these stations may therefore be compared with that of the two sections.

The mean temperature (100—400 metres) of Mohn's stations is 2.84° C.

The mean temperature of Isachsen's Stats. 2, 3, 4, 5, 7, 8, 9, 10, and 11, is 3.07° C. As Stats. 5 and 7 are farther west than any of Mohn's stations, they might be left out; but this will make no appreciable difference in the mean temperature.

As the observations at Isachsen's stations were taken about 34 days earlier in the season than those at Mohn's stations, their mean temperature might be increased to 3.41° C. in order to be comparable with the mean temperature of the latter. The water of the current should accordingly have been about 0.57° C. colder in 1878 than in 1910. This agrees fairly

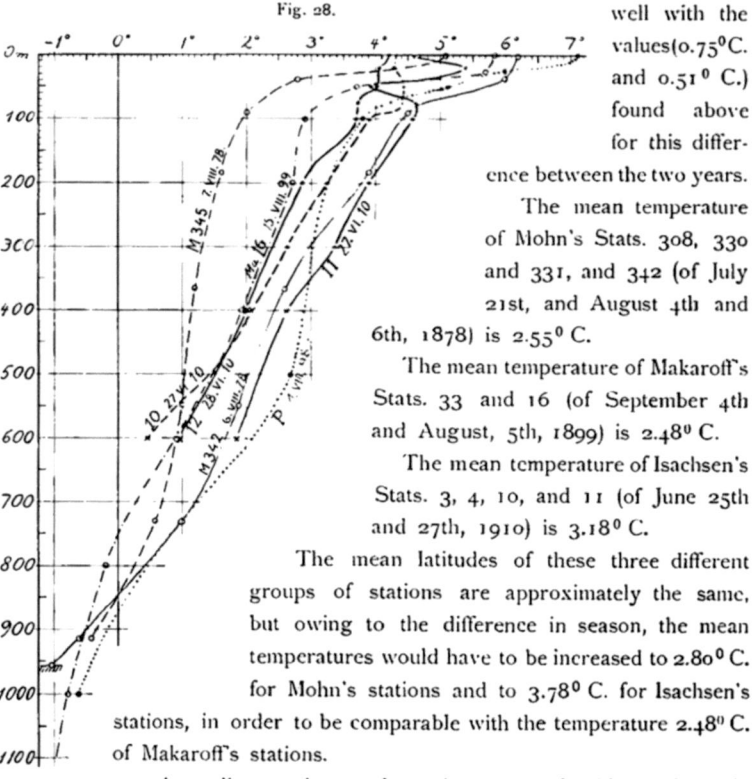

Fig. 28.

well with the values (0.75° C. and 0.51° C.) found above for this difference between the two years.

The mean temperature of Mohn's Stats. 308, 330 and 331, and 342 (of July 21st, and August 4th and 6th, 1878) is 2.55° C.

The mean temperature of Makaroff's Stats. 33 and 16 (of September 4th and August, 5th, 1899) is 2.48° C.

The mean temperature of Isachsen's Stats. 3, 4, 10, and 11 (of June 25th and 27th, 1910) is 3.18° C.

The mean latitudes of these three different groups of stations are approximately the same, but owing to the difference in season, the mean temperatures would have to be increased to 2.80° C. for Mohn's stations and to 3.78° C. for Isachsen's stations, in order to be comparable with the temperature 2.48° C. of Makaroff's stations.

According to these values, the current should have been, in 1910, 1.30° C. warmer than in 1899, and 0.98° C. warmer than in 1878.

The mean temperature of Mohn's Stats. 306 and 308 is 2.22° C., that of Isachsen's Stats. 3 and 4 is 3.07° C., and that of Makaroff's Stat. 33 is 2.52° C. The first four of these were south of the last (see Fig. 21) but taken earlier in the season. If we compensate for this, the mean temperature of Mohn's stations should be 2.57° C., and of Isachsen's stations 3.70° C. The current in 1910 should consequently have been 1.18° C. warmer than in 1899, and 1.13° C. warmer than in 1878.

The mean temperature of Makaroff's Stat. 16 (of August 15th, 1899) was 2.45° C. That of Isachsen's Stats. 10 and 11 (of June 27th, 1910) was 3.28° C., which, owing to the earlier season, should be increased to 3.75° C. The current should accordingly have been 1.30° C. warmer in 1910 than in 1899.

The curve of Hamberg's Stat. U. of September 1, 1898, (Fig. 24), compared with the curves of Isachsen's Stats. 1 and 11, and Makaroff's

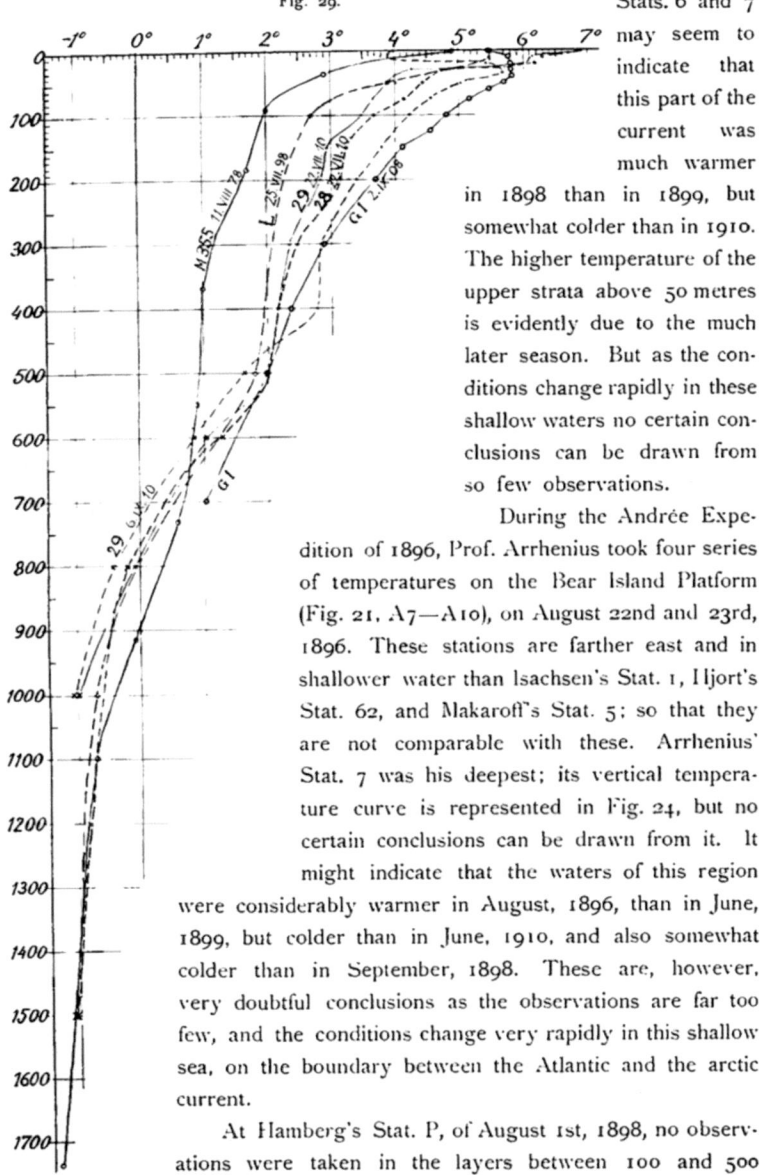

Fig. 29.

Stats. 6 and 7 may seem to indicate that this part of the current was much warmer in 1898 than in 1899, but somewhat colder than in 1910. The higher temperature of the upper strata above 50 metres is evidently due to the much later season. But as the conditions change rapidly in these shallow waters no certain conclusions can be drawn from so few observations.

During the Andrée Expedition of 1896, Prof. Arrhenius took four series of temperatures on the Bear Island Platform (Fig. 21, A7—A10), on August 22nd and 23rd, 1896. These stations are farther east and in shallower water than Isachsen's Stat. 1, Hjort's Stat. 62, and Makaroff's Stat. 5; so that they are not comparable with these. Arrhenius' Stat. 7 was his deepest; its vertical temperature curve is represented in Fig. 24, but no certain conclusions can be drawn from it. It might indicate that the waters of this region were considerably warmer in August, 1896, than in June, 1899, but colder than in June, 1910, and also somewhat colder than in September, 1898. These are, however, very doubtful conclusions as the observations are far too few, and the conditions change very rapidly in this shallow sea, on the boundary between the Atlantic and the arctic current.

At Hamberg's Stat. P, of August 1st, 1898, no observations were taken in the layers between 100 and 500 metres. The mean temperature of 100 to 400 metres, has therefore to be taken from the vertical temperature-curve (see Fig. 28) which cannot be very accurate. According to this, the mean temperature should be about $3.25°$ C.

The mean temperature of Isachsen's Stats. 10, 11 and 12, of June 27th—28th, 1910, is 3.09^0 C. Owing to the earlier season, this should be raised to 3.42^0 C. in order to be comparable with that of Hamberg's station.

The current should accordingly have been about 0.17^0 C. warmer in 1910 than in 1898.

The mean temperature of Stat. 1 (Fig. 21, G 1) of the De Geer Expedition, on September 2nd, 1908, was 3.44^0 C. (see the following Table).

	G 1 2. IX. 08	29 6. IX. 10	28 & 29 22. VII. 10	M 353, 354, 355 10. VIII. 78	26, 27, 28, 29 22. VII. 10	L 25. VII. 98
100	4.8^0 C.	4.23^0 C.	3.55^0 C.	1.08^0 C.	3.56^0 C.	2.68^0 C.
200	3.7	3.40	3.00	1.05	2.8	2.25
300	2.9	2.84	2.41	0.85	2.2	2.07
400	2.37	2.77	2.29	0.73	1.95	1.95
Mean	3.44	3.31	2.81	0.93	2.63	2.24

The mean temperature of Isachsen's Stat. 29, of September 6th, 1910, was 3.31^0 C. That of his Stats. 28 and 29 of July 22nd, 1910, was 2.81^0 C. Owing to the earlier season, this should be raised to 3.26^0 C. in order to be comparable with the former.

Owing to the more southerly position the mean temperature of G 1 should be raised to 3.54^0 C.

In this region the Current should accordingly have been about 0.25^0 C. warmer in 1908 than in 1910.

The mean temperature of Mohn's Stats. 353, 354, and 355 was 0.93^0 C., while that of Isachsen's Stats. 26, 27, 28, and 29 was 2.63^0 C. Owing to the difference in latitude and in season, the latter value should be corrected to 2.78^0 C.

According to these values, the current should have been 1.85^0 C. colder in 1878 than in 1910.

Owing to the more northerly position, the mean temperature (2.24^0 C.) of Hamberg's Stat. L, of July 25th, 1898, should be corrected to 2.30^0 C. in order to be comparable with the mean temperature 2.81^0 C. of Stats. 28 and 29 of July 22nd, 1910.

The current should accordingly have been 0.51^0 C. colder in 1898 than in 1910.

Arrhenius' Stations 3—6 of August 21st, 1896, (Fig. 21, A 3—A 6), are north of Isachsen's Section VI. Unfortunately, however, the deep-sea

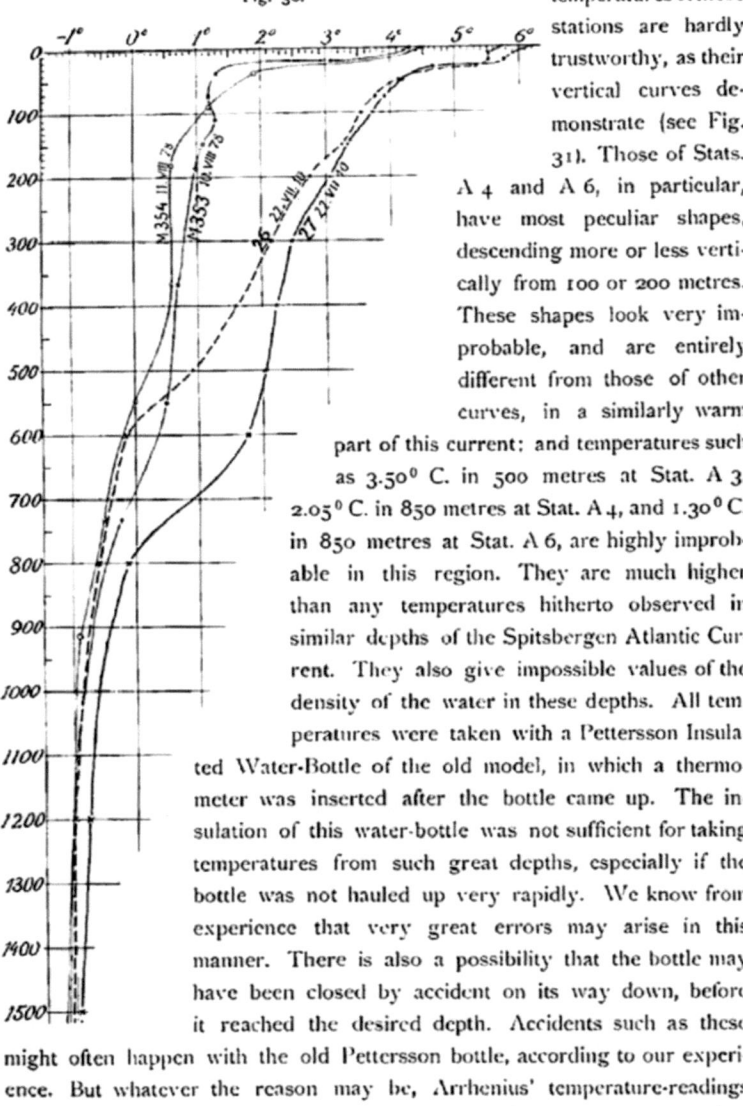

Fig. 30.

temperatures of these stations are hardly trustworthy, as their vertical curves demonstrate (see Fig. 31). Those of Stats. A 4 and A 6, in particular, have most peculiar shapes, descending more or less vertically from 100 or 200 metres. These shapes look very improbable, and are entirely different from those of other curves, in a similarly warm part of this current: and temperatures such as 3.50° C. in 500 metres at Stat. A 3, 2.05° C. in 850 metres at Stat. A 4, and 1.30° C. in 850 metres at Stat. A 6, are highly improbable in this region. They are much higher than any temperatures hitherto observed in similar depths of the Spitsbergen Atlantic Current. They also give impossible values of the density of the water in these depths. All temperatures were taken with a Pettersson Insulated Water-Bottle of the old model, in which a thermometer was inserted after the bottle came up. The insulation of this water-bottle was not sufficient for taking temperatures from such great depths, especially if the bottle was not hauled up very rapidly. We know from experience that very great errors may arise in this manner. There is also a possibility that the bottle may have been closed by accident on its way down, before it reached the desired depth. Accidents such as these might often happen with the old Pettersson bottle, according to our experience. But whatever the reason may be, Arrhenius' temperature-readings cannot at any rate be considered trustworthy for depths greater than 300 metres.

By using the vertical temperature-curves of his four stations represented in Fig. 31, and trying to correct for the most obvious errors, we have found a mean temperature for 100, 200, 300, and 400 metres, of 2.1° C.

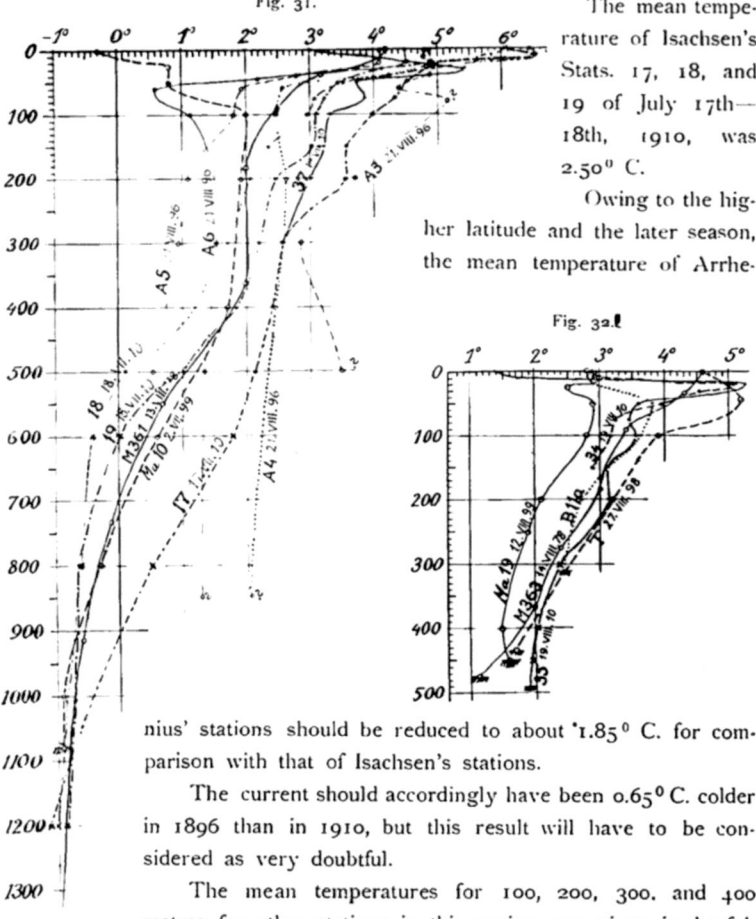

Fig. 31.

Fig. 32.

The mean temperature of Isachsen's Stats. 17, 18, and 19 of July 17th—18th, 1910, was 2.50° C.

Owing to the higher latitude and the later season, the mean temperature of Arrhenius' stations should be reduced to about 1.85° C. for comparison with that of Isachsen's stations.

The current should accordingly have been 0.65° C. colder in 1896 than in 1910, but this result will have to be considered as very doubtful.

The mean temperatures for 100, 200, 300, and 400 metres for other stations in this region, are given in the following table:[1]

	17 & 18 17. VII. 10	A 3 & A 4 21. VIII. 96	M 361 13. VIII. 78	Ma 10 2. VII. 99	37 19. VIII. 10	B 3 10. VI. 05
Mean t° C.	2.56° C	2.92° C.?	2.03° C.	1.85° C.	2.79° C.	2.44° C.
Corrected to July 17th.	2.56	2.68 ?	1.88	2.00	2.60	3.00

[1] At Isachsen's Stat. 37 and the Belgica Stat. 3 (B 3), the temperature in 400 metres had to be taken from the probable vertical temperature-curves.

According to the corrected values in the lower line of this table, the current in 1878 was 0.68° C., in 1899 0.58° C. lower than in 1910, while in 1905 it should have been 0.40° C. and in 1896 0.12° C. warmer than in 1910.

The following table gives the mean temperatures at four stations in the northernmost region of the Spitsbergen Atlantic Current where it runs over the submarine ridge into the North Polar Basin. As the depth at the Belgica Station 11a was only 310 metres, a probable temperature had to be assumed for 400 metres, in accordance with the various vertical temperature-curves (see Fig. 32).

	35 19. VIII. 10	M 363 14. VIII. 78	Ma 19 13. VIII. 99	T 27. VIII. 98	B 11 a 7. VII. 05
Mean t° C. 100—400 m.	2.78° C.	2.57° C.	2.03° C.	2.89° C.	2.70° C.
Corrected to Aug. 19th	2.78	2.63	2.09	2.81	3.13

In 1878 the current should accordingly have been 0.15° C., and in 1899 0.69° C. colder than in 1910, while in 1898 it should have been 0.03° C. and in 1905 0.35° C. warmer than in 1910. But nothing certain can be concluded in this respect from observations from single stations in a region where the sea is so shallow, and where the waters differ so much within short distances.

In the following table we have computed the means of the above analyses of the temperatures of the Spitsbergen Atlantic Current in different years. All mean temperatures have been referred to the corrected mean temperature of the current in the same region in 1910. Where the mean temperature for one year was lower than that of 1910, the difference is given in the table with the minus sign; where it was higher, the difference is marked with plus.

As there is such a great distance between the most southern and the most northern stations that we have examined, we cannot consider the water examined in the same summer in these widely-separated regions as water of quite the same year. The water examined in Isachsen's Sect. VI, for instance, has evidently come through the Færoe-Shetland Channel into the Norwegian Sea long before the water examined in Sect. I. We have therefore divided the area examined into a southern region of Isachsen's Sections I and II, and a northern region of Isachsen's Sections IV and VI.

	1878	1896	1898	1899	1900	1901	1905	1908	1910
Region of Sects. I & II	−0.79	− ?	−0.17	−1.12	−1.34	−0.6			0.00
Region of Sects. IV & VI	−0.89	−0.27	−0.24	−0.64			+0.38	+0.25	0.00

The material of observations is naturally much too small for a computation of the normal temperature of the water of the current in these regions. It is, however, evident that the water was comparatively very warm in 1910, and the above values have, therefore, to be raised by a certain amount, in order to give more probable values for the anomaly. If it be assumed that the anomaly of the temperature of the water in 1910 was $+0.40°$ C. in the southern region (of Sects. I and II), and $+0.25°$ C. in the northern region (of Sects. IV and VI), we find the following values of the possible anomaly in the other years:

	1878	1896	1898	1899	1900	1901	1905	1908	1910
Region of Sects. I & II	−0.39	+ ?	+0.23	−0.72	−0.94	−0.2			+0.40
Region of Sects. IV & VI	−0.64	−0.02	+0.01	−0.39			+0.63	+0.50	+0.25

The above values are naturally very inaccurate as they are based on far too few observations. They may therefore only be considered as giving some approximate indications of the directions in which the variations of the temperature of the current have gone in some years. The values may be considered as most trustworthy for 1878, 1900, and 1910, from which years we have the fullest and best material of observations. From 1899 there are also a good many observations, though scattered over a wide area and giving no vertical sections of the current. The observations from 1898 are very few and insufficient for comparison, from 1908 there is only one vertical series of observations, and from 1901 there are no deeper observations than in 200 and 280 metres. The observations from 1896 are not satisfactory for a comparison such as this.

From 1905 there are only two stations, taken during the Belgica expedition very far north; and no certain conclusions can be drawn from them as to the mean temperature of the current that year. The anomaly found. $+0.63°$ C., agrees nevertheless very well with the fact that the Norwegian Atlantic Current was very warm in the Lofoten section in May, 1904, and in the Sognefjord section in May, 1903.

In our memoir on the Norwegian Sea [1909] we put forth as an experiment the supposition that the water of the Atlantic Current may spend approximately one year in travelling from the region of our Sognefjord-section to the region of our Lofoten-section.

Our calculations and conclusions based upon this supposition gave very reasonable results. It seems probable, however, that the greater part of the water of the current may travel somewhat farther than this distance in the period of one year. We do not, however, consider it probable that water passing the Sognefjord-section in one year will on the average reach the region of Isachsen's Sect. VI, or say 79^0 N. Lat., much earlier than two years later, leaving out of consideration the possibly more rapid drift of surface-water. These same slowly-moving water-masses must naturally reach the region of Isachsen's Sections I and II in a shorter period, perhaps nearly half a year less. If it be assumed that they spend two years in travelling from about 62^0 N. Lat. (the Sognefjord-section) to 79^0 N. Lat., it would follow that they would need about 5 months less to reach the region of Isachsen's Sect. I, in 75^0 N. Lat.

We found [1909, pp. 193 *et seq.*] that the variations in the mean temperature of the Atlantic water of the Sognefjord-section in May, each year, was to some extent followed by similar variations in the mean temperature of the atmosphere in Norway in the winters following. If this be correct, and if the variations in the mean temperature of the Spitsbergen Atlantic Current, near 79^0 N. Lat., be approximately similar to those of the temperature of the Sognefjord-section two years earlier, we may expect some kind of agreement between these variations of the Spitsbergen Current, and the variations in the winter-temperature of the preceding winters.

The following table gives the mean anomalies of the temperatures for the period from December 1st to May 31st, of various years, for all 22 meteorological stations of Norway, and the corresponding anomalies for the five northern stations, Tromso, Andenes, Alten, Vardo and Sydvaranger, compared with the possible anomalies of the mean temperature of the Spitsbergen Current in the summer a year and a half later:

Dec. 1 — May 31	Mean Anomaly of Air-Temperature of		Possible Anomaly of Temperature of Spitsbergen Current		
	22 Stations in Norway	Five Northern Stations	Year	Region of Sects. IV & VI	Region of Sects. I & II
1876—77	—2.13	—1.78	1878	—0.64	—0.39
1877—78	1.27	1.53			
1894—95	—0.22	—0.02	1896	—0.02	+ ?
1895—96	1.33	1.83			
1896—97	0.25	1.08	1898	0.01	0.23
1897—98	1.00	0.82	1899	—0.39	—0.72
1898—99	—0.73	—2.44	1900		—0.94
1899—1900	—1.28	—0.98	1901		—0.2
1900—01	0.30	0.46			
1903—04	0.35	1.35	1905	0.63	
1904—05	0.55	0.25			
1906—07	1.12	1.11	1908	0.50	
1907—08	0.48	0.30			
1908—09	0.12	0.68	1910	0.25	0.40
1909—10	1.25	1.61			

The variations in the anomalies of the temperature of the Current in the northern region (of Sects. IV and VI) agree fairly well with the variations in the winter-temperature of the whole of Norway, and still better with those in the winter-temperature of the five northern stations. The most striking exception is the temperature of the current of 1899, which is comparatively too low. The agreement may seem surprising, considering the very imperfect observation-material on which our calculation of the anomalies of the current is based.

The variations in the anomalies of the temperature of the current in the southern region of Sects. I and II do not agree so well with the variations in the winter-temperature a year and a half before. Considering, however, that the waters in this region have spent less time on their way from the south — perhaps five months less, but not so much less that their temperatures may be comparable with the winter-temperature of Norway in the preceding winter of the same year, *i. e.* one year later than the others — it might seem reasonable to compare them with the means of the air-temperature of the two preceding winters. This is done in the following table:

Dec. 1 – May 31	Mean Anomaly of Air-Temperature of		Year	Anomaly of Temperature of Spitsbergen Current of Southern region of Sects. I & II
	22 Stations of Norway	Five northern Stations		
1876–77 and 1877–78	−0.43	−0.13	1878	−0.39
1894–95 „ 1895–06	0.56	0.91	1896	+ ?
1896–97 „ 1897–98	0.63	0.95	1898	0.23
1897–98 „ 1898–99	0.14	−0.81	1899	−0.72
1898–99 „ 1899–1900	−1.01	−1.71	1900	−0.94
1899–1900 „ 1900–01	−0.49	−0.26	1901	−0.2(?)
1908–09 „ 1909–10	0.69	1.15	1910	0.40

In this table there is a very fair agreement, especially between the variations in the anomalies of the five northern stations of Norway and the variations in the hypothetical anomalies of the temperature of the Spitsbergen Current in the southern region of Isachsen's Sections (Sects. I and II).

Curves demonstrating the variations in the above-mentioned anomalies are represented in Figs. 33 and 34. The agreement between these

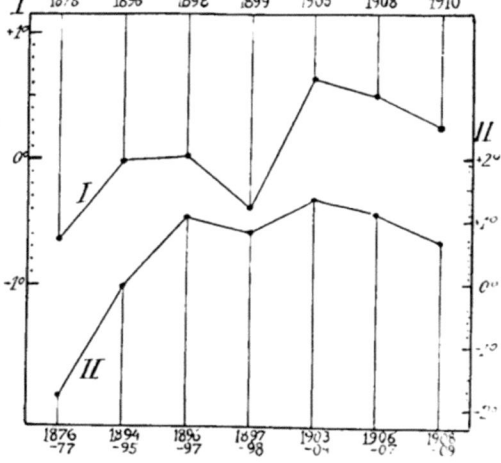

Fig. 33. Curve I. Temperature-Anomaly of Spitsbergen Atlantic Current off northern west coast of Spitsbergen (scale to the left). Curve II: Mean Anomaly of Air-Temperature during the winter (from Dec. 1 to May 31) at the five northern Meteorological Stations of Norway (scale to the right).

curves is striking, especially considering the very imperfect observation-material upon which the curves of the Spitsbergen Current are based.

It seems as if the results of this investigation of the variations in the temperature of the Spitsbergen Atlantic Current compared with the variations in the winter-temperature of Norway is a remarkably good verification of the correctness of our views held forth in our memoir on the Norwegian Sea [1909] as to the close relation between the temperature of the Atlantic Current in the southern Norwegian Sea and the air-temperature of the following winter in Norway.

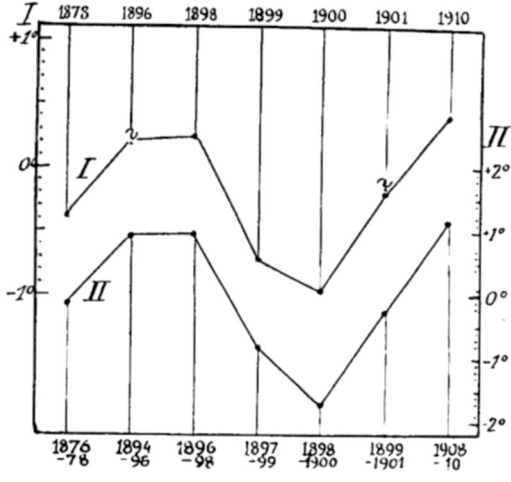

Fig. 34. Curve I: Temperature-Anomaly of Spitsbergen Atlantic Current in southern region between Bear Island and southern Spitsbergen (scale to the left). Curve II: Mean Anomaly of Air-Temperature during the two preceding winters (from Dec. 1 to May 31) at the five northern Meteorological Stations of Norway (scale to the right).

The above variations found in the temperature of the Spitsbergen Atlantic Current also agree with the variations in the distribution of ice in the Barents and Spitsbergen Seas, as far as we know them. In our memoir on the Norwegian Sea [1909, pp. 189 et seq.] it was pointed out that the annual variations in the distribution of ice in the Barents Sea in May seem to agree to some extent with the variations in the temperature of the Atlantic Current in the Lofoten section one year earlier, and in the Sognefjord section two years earlier. We might then expect a similar agreement between these variations in the distribution of the ice and the variations in the temperature of the Spitsbergen Current of the same year, because the water will probably need about the same time to reach the central region of the Barents Sea and the northern region west of Spitsbergen. The following table gives the areas of open water in the Barents Sea east of 20° E. Long. in May, and the anomalies of the temperature of the Spitsbergen Current in the same years. For 1900 and 1901 we had to use the values from the southern region of the current; this may perhaps be the explanation why the values of these years do not agree as well as the others.

	1900	1901	1905	1908	1910
Thousands of Square Kilometres of open water in the Barents Sea in May	440	398	639	568	492
Anomaly of the Temperature of the Spitsbergen Current	−0.94	−0.2 ?	0.63	0.50	0.25

Considering the very inaccurate methods, and the insufficient observation-material at our disposal, a better agreement cannot be expected. The variations seem to have gone in the same direction, as is demonstrated by the curves in Fig. 35.

It might seem probable that the distribution of the ice in the sea west of Spitsbergen is also more or less dependent on the variations in the Spitsbergen Atlantic Current. But in this deep sea it is evidently less dependent on the temperature of the water than in the shallow Barents Sea, and is more dependent on the distribution of the currents, and on the prevailing winds.

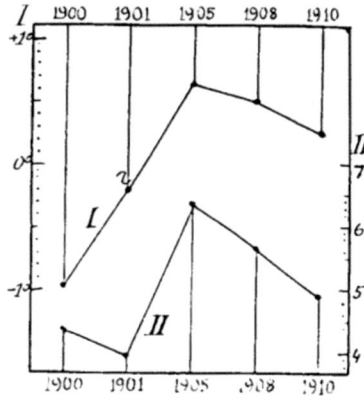

Fig. 35. Curve I: Temperature-Anomaly of Spitsbergen Atlantic Current (scale to the left). Curve II: The Area (in hundred-thousands of square kilometres) of open water in the Barents Sea in May (scale to the right).

We have previously [1909, pp. 204, *et seq.*] pointed out that there is probably a close relation between the annual variations in the temperature of the Norwegian Atlantic Current and the growth and spawning of the food-fishes; and we found especially that the Lofoten fisheries had corresponding variations. When the Atlantic Current had a comparatively high temperature in the Sognefjord-section (northeast of the Færoe-Shetland Channel) in May of one year the fisheries began late at Lofoten in the following winter, and the cod was in a comparatively poor condition, *e. g.* with small liver; and vice versa if the current was cold. We might consequently expect that there should be a somewhat similar agreement between the annual variations of the temperature of the Spitsbergen Atlantic Current and the variations of the Lofoten fisheries of each preceding year.

The curves of Fig. 36 represent the variations in the temperature of the Spitsbergen Atlantic Current in different years, in the northern region (Curve I) as found above[1], the variations in the mean anomaly of the winter temperature (December—May) a year and a half earlier at the five northern meteorological Stations of Norway (Curve II), and the variations in the quantity of cod-liver in hectolitres per 1000 fish, fished at Lofoten in each previous year (Curve III).

---

[1] For 1900 and 1901 we had to use values from the southern region.

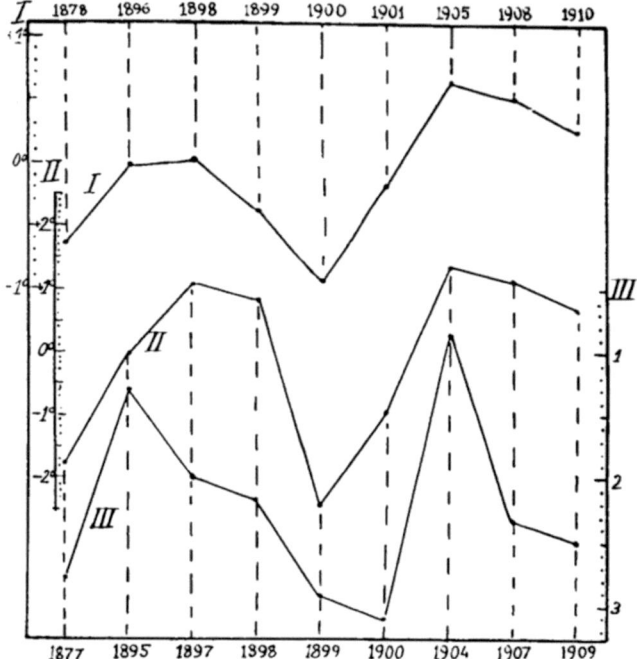

Fig. 36. Curve I: Temperature-Anomaly of Spitsbergen Atlantic Current (scale I to the left). Curve II: Mean anomaly of the Winter-Temperature (Dec.—May) at the five northern Meteorological Stations of Norway (scale II to the left). Curve III: Quantity of Cod-liver (in Hectolitres per 1000 fish) obtained during the Lofoten Fisheries (scale III to the right).

The agreement between these curves is better than might be expected, considering the insufficiency of the observation-material at our disposal.

The "Waves" of the Equilines of the Sections.

The equilines demonstrate in Sections I, II, IV, and VI the same kind of undulations or "waves" as we have frequently observed in sections of the Atlantic Current off the Norwegian coast, and which we have discussed at length in our work on the Norwegian Sea [cf. 1909, pp. 87 *et seq.*]. These "waves" in the sections may either be due to some kind of periodical or unperiodical vertical movements of the water-strata, or they may indicate some kind of horizontal movements or vortex-movements of the water-masses.

In the former case one might expect that they had some connection with the tidal wave, producing periodical variations in the Ocean currents, which would again cause periodical displacements of the water-strata.

Provided that the relation between the velocities of the movements of the upper and lower water-strata of the northward-flowing Atlantic Current, off the west coast of Spitsbergen, changed considerably with the tidal wave, this would necessarily have a great effect upon the depth of the various strata at the sides of the current, owing to the deflecting force caused by the Earth's rotation, by which the northward-moving water is pressed against the continental slope off Spitsbergen. It has to be considered that this deflecting force increases with the sinus of the latitude, and is very great in these northern regions. Another circumstance of importance is also that the direction of the tidal currents is continually changing during the day and night, and sometimes they may be directed transversally to the sections, and at other times more or less parallel to them. It seems therefore probable that the tidal currents must have some influence upon the position of the isohalines and isotherms, but how much it is difficult to decide at present.

It may be of interest to find out what intervals of time there are between the observations at the various stations, and in what relation they stood to the position of the moon.

The curves in Figs. 37 and 38 represent a hypothetical period of the same length as the time between the upper and lower culminations of the moon, which are indicated respectively by rings and black discs. The date and the hours of the day (from 1 to 24 from midnight to midnight) are given along the abscissa. The duration of the observations at each station is indicated by small rings on the curves, and the number of the station is written above them. If these curves be compared with the Sections I, II, IV and VI (Pls. IV and V), it is seen that the observations at those stations where the most conspicuous "waves" occur, actually coincide with those parts of the curves where they might be expected, if the "waves" be due to some vertical periodical movement of this kind.

The most conspicuous "waves" occur in Sections VI and IV. The tops of these "waves" are at Stats. 16, 18 (perhaps also

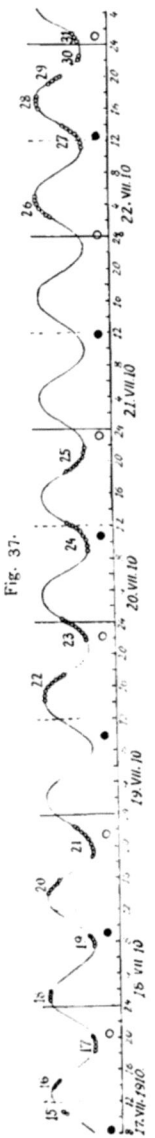

Fig. 37.

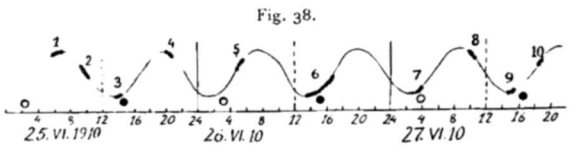

Fig. 38.

20), 26, and 28 (perhaps also 29). The observations at all these stations are also near the tops of the "waves" of the curve in Fig. 37. On the other hand the valleys of the "waves" of the Sections are at Stats. 17, 19 (perhaps 21), 25, 27, and perhaps 30. The observations at all these stations are in the valleys of the curve in Fig. 37. There is actually no exception from the rule: for the other stations (*viz.* Stats. 15, 20, 21, 22, 23, 24, and 31) cannot be counted, as they are more or less outside the area of the Atlantic Current, and their vertical distribution of temperature and salinity was such that vertical movements of the water-strata would not make much difference.

In Sections I and II there are no very conspicuous "waves" of the same kind as in Sects. IV and VI [1]. But there are indications of some "waves," *e. g.* perhaps at Stats. 7, 8, 9, 10, and 11, where the isotherms demonstrate undulations. And in these cases there is actually also agreement with the tidal curve in Fig. 38. The great rise of the isohaline of 35.0 $^0/_{00}$ at Stats. 9 and 10, is evidently a phenomenon different from the above-mentioned waves, this being also proved by the fact that the isotherms have no similar rise.

On the whole the results of the above analysis may seem to be in favour of the view that there is some connection between the "waves" in the sections and the tidal phenomena. Our discussion of the subject in our work on the Norwegian Sea [1909, p. 97] led to similar conclusions, one of them being that at any rate some "waves" in the vertical sections of the Norwegian Sea had some connection with the tidal phenomena. It is not to be expected, however, that the period of these "waves" would be exactly the same as that of the moon; and therefore it is not probable that there would be perfect agreement between them. But as the material of observations at hand is hardly sufficient for a satisfactory study of this question, it is not worth while to go farther into detail here.

The Branches of the Spitsbergen Atlantic Current.

The observations of the Spitsbergen Expedition of 1910 in connection with those of the Belgica Expedition of 1905 demonstrate very clearly the courses and extension of the branches given off from the Spitsbergen Atlantic Current — the branch flowing westward and forming the inter-

---

[1] Sections I and II were taken between June 25th and 27th, three to five days after spring tide, the full moon occurring on June 22nd. Sections VI and IV were taken from July 17th to 23rd, from five days before till one day after spring tide. It seems therefore hardly probable that there would have been much difference in this respect; for it is not credible that, for instance, the tidal wave should have been bigger at Stat. 18 on July 18th, four days before full moon, than at Stat. 3 on June 25th, three days after full moon.

mediate warm layer under the East Greenland Polar Current [cf. HELLAND-HANSEN and KOEFOED, 1909, pp. 309 *et seq.*, 319; HELLAND-HANSEN and NANSEN, 1909, pp. 280 *et seq.*, 317 *et seq.*], as well as the branch flowing northward into the North Polar Basin and forming the intermediate warm layer there [cf. NANSEN, 1902 and 1906; HELLAND-HANSEN and KOEFOED, 1909, pp. 308 *et seq.*].

The Westward Branch. Sections IV, V and VI and our maps for 50, 100, 200 and 300 metres prove that this branch flows westward in the region of Stats. 22 and 21, in about 77^0 40′ and 78^0 N. Lat., while Stats. 23 and 24 are situated in the cold central area of this sea [cf. NANSEN, 1906]. This agrees remarkably well with the observations during the Belgica Expedition of 1905 and with our previous maps of the current. At the Belgica Station 23, in 77^0 25′ N. and 4^0 3′ E. the water of this branch was forming an intermediate layer between 100 and 400 metres, with salinities between 35.00 and 34.95 $^0/_{00}$. As the branch, according to our view [cf. 1909], should run southwestward in this region, we also find that the waters of the current were farther north in about 77^0 40′ and 78^0 N. in the region of Isachsen's Stats. 22 and 21, than farther west in the region of the Belgica Station 23. The resemblance between our present maps for 50 and 100, and 200 metres (Pls. II and III) and our earlier maps [HELLAND-HANSEN and KOEFOED, 1909, Pls. LXIII, LXIV, HELLAND-HANSEN and NANSEN, 1909, p. 283, Fig. 93] is striking; but the vertical Section IV of 1910, shows that the current is broader west of Spitsbergen than we had previously thought. Hamberg's Stats. N and O of the Nathorst Expedition 1898 [HAMBERG, 1906] were in 77^0 52′ N., 3^0 5′ W. and in 78^0 13′ N., 2^0 58′ W. Hamberg found there water of the same current, probably with salinities about 35.00 $^0/_{00}$ [cf. our remarks 1909, p. 280], in 100 and 500 metres, while his Stat. M., in 77^0 39′ N., 1^0 18′ E., was evidently on the boundary of the cold central area, and had only a slight indication at 200 metres of the waters of the warm, saline current. The observations at these stations consequently indicate very nearly the same conditions in this region in 1898 as in 1910.

The Frithjof Station 1, of July 8th, 1900 (in 77^0 11′ N., 2^0 58 W.), was some distance to the west of Stat. 23 of 1910 and southeast of the Belgica Station 23 of 1905. There was observed comparatively warm and saline water in 100, 200 and 300 metres [cf. our mention of it, 1909, p. 280], a circumstance which also agrees remarkably well with all the other observations. We have thus observations from four different years — 1898, 1900, 1905, and 1910—which agree, and we may conclude that this branch of the Spitsbergen Atlantic Current flows regularly westward and southwestward in this region.

The Northward Branch. Sections VI, VII, and VIII of July and August, 1910, in connection with the observations at the Belgica stations to the north and northwest, prove that a narrow tongue of water with salinities about and slightly above 35.0 °/oo (*viz.* 35.02 °/oo in 200 metres at Stat. 37 of 1910, and 35.01 °/oo at the Belgica Stats. 11 a and 12, in 100 to 300 metres) extends northwards along the northern Spitsbergen coast at depths between 100 or 150 metres and 300 or 400 metres. This water probably flows into the North Polar Basin along the slope of the continental shelf trending northeast and eastward north of Spitsbergen. According to what has been said above (p. 17) about the gradual decrease of the salinity of the Spitsbergen Atlantic Current during its northward course, we do not consider it probable that as a rule the maximum salinity of this northward branch, entering the North Polar Basin, much exceeds the above values 35.01 and 35.02 °/oo [1]. We therefore consider this to be the probable upper limit of the salinity of the intermediate, comparatively warm water-layers of the North Polar Basin, below 200 metres, formed by this inflowing water. By a careful analysis of the determinations during the Fram Expedition, Nansen [1906, pp. 99 *et seq.*] came to the conclusion that the salinity of this water, as well as of the bottom-water of the North Polar Basin, should be about 35.08 and 35.10 °/oo. We think that the later researches of the Belgica Expedition and the Isachsen Expedition make it highly improbable that salinities as high as these occur in the intermediate layer of this Basin, and we therefore think that even Nansen's corrected values must have been too high.

According to the observations at the Belgica stations in the north, it seems probable that the greater part of the water carried by the northward continuation of the Spitsbergen Atlantic Current into the North Polar Basin has salinities between 34.95 °/oo and 35.0 °/oo.

---

[1] This might seem to be contradicted by the fact that at Hamberg's Stat. T, of Aug. 27, 1898, in 79^0 58' N., 9^0 35' E., he found salinities of 35.17 °/oo in 45—200 metres and 35.12 °/oo in 435 metres. As before mentioned, his values are too high, as is proved by his salinities of the cold bottom-water; but even if the above values be reduced by 0.10 °/oo which was found to be the probable error at other stations, we obtain salinities of 35.07 °/oo, which seems very high.

The Bottom-Water.

The temperatures observed in the bottom-water at the stations of the Isachsen Expedition agree on the whole very well with those observed during the Belgica Expedition in 1905, and by Roald Amundsen in 1901.

In the region investigated by Amundsen, where the bottom-water is formed at the surface, he observed, with his Richter reversing thermometer, temperatures of -1.30 and $-1.26°$ C. at 2000 metres.

At the Belgica stations (23—26) in the region west of Isachsen's Section IV, between $76° 28'$ and $77° 25'$ N., temperatures between -1.28 and $-1.30°$ C. were observed near the bottom in depths between 2300 and 3000 metres, and at Stat. 27 a, a temperature of $-1.31°$ C. was observed at 1700 metres, 30 metres above the bottom.

The observations in 2000 metres at the Isachsen stations were not so close to the bottom, and it is not therefore to be expected that they would give such low temperatures as the above. The one which was probably nearest to the bottom was at Stat. 27 (see Sect. IV). The temperature observed was $-1.28°$ C. which agrees remarkably well with the above bottom-temperatures of the Belgica Expedition, and also with those of Amundsen. At Stat. 26 a temperature of $-1.26°$ C. was observed at 2000 metres which, however, was evidently not so near to the bottom as that of Stat. 27, but probably nearer than those of the other stations. The other observations in 2000 metres at the stations of 1910 gave higher temperatures, between -1.15 and $-1.24°$ C. (See Fig. 39).

The salinities of the bottom-water found at the Isachsen stations vary between 34.87 and $34.93°/_{00}$, but are on the whole comparatively low, being to a great extent between 34.88 and 34.90 in depths exceeding 1200 metres. As a rule they are especially low where the temperatures are low; and where the temperature is below $-1.15°$ C. the salinity is below $34.90°/_{00}$ except at Stats. 25 and 26, where the salinity was found to be 34.92 and $34.91°/_{00}$ with temperatures of -1.17 and $-1.26°$ C. at 2000 metres. The low salinities with the low temperatures agree well with Amundsen's observations, the salinities at his stations for depths exceeding 1000 metres varying between 34.88 and $34.93°/_{00}$, but being most frequently 34.90 and $34.89°/_{00}$, with temperatures about $-1.3°$ C.

The salinities of the cold bottom-water at the Belgica stations are most frequently $34.92°/_{00}$, and in a few cases 34.91 and $34.90°/_{00}$. There are, however, no observations of the salinity at greater depths than 1800 metres, and it is possible that somewhat lower values would have been found at the greater depths near the bottom where the temperature sank to -1.28

and 1.30° C., which would be more in accordance with the salinities at the Amundsen stations and the Isachsen stations. It seems, however, as if the salinities of the bottom-water have on the whole had a tendency to be somewhat higher at the Belgica stations than at the Amundsen stations

Fig. 39. Observations of the Bottom-water at 2000 (and 1800) metres, during the Michael Sars Exp. 1900, the Amundsen Exp. 1901, the Belgica Exp. 1905 (at 1800 metres), and the Isachsen Exp. 1910.

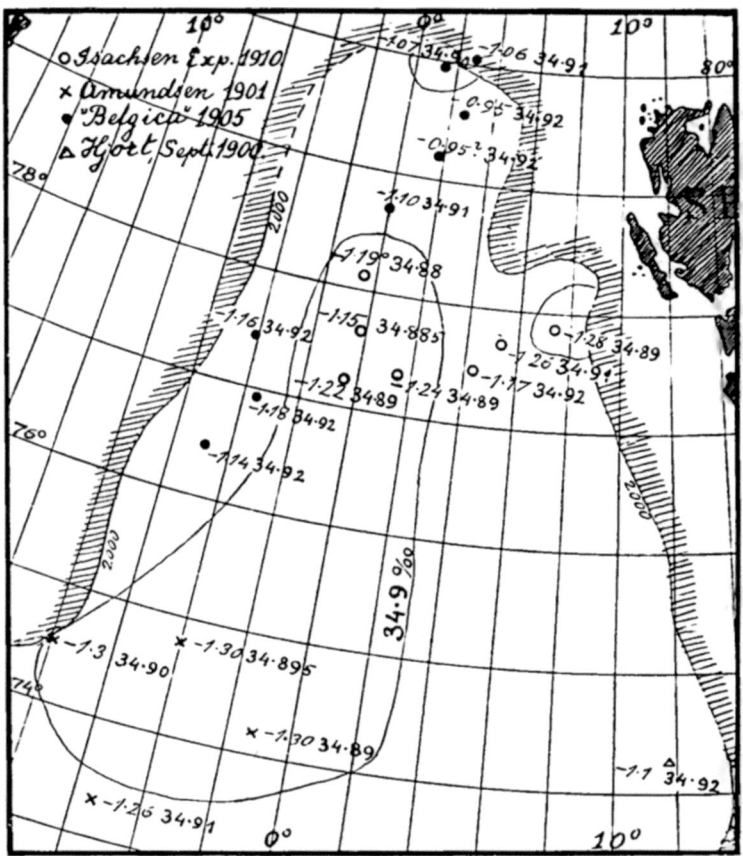

to the south, and the Isachsen stations to the east (cf. Figs. 39 and 40). Whether this is due to slight differences which really have existed in the sea, or to slight differences in the titrations, cannot be decided.

From what has been pointed out above, we may possibly draw the conclusion that the bottom-water, when it is formed in the region of Amundsen's stations, has at 2000 metres a temperature of about — 1.30° C.

(corresponding to about $-1.39°$ C. at the surface) and a salinity of between 34.87 and 34.90 $°/_{00}$. This water, with a density (σ_t) of about 28.10, spreads slowly along the bottom of the sea outwards from this region. By intermixture with overlying waters the temperature as well as the

Fig. 40. Observations of the Bottom-water at 1200 metres, during the Amundsen Exp. in 1901, the Belgica Exp. in 1905 and the Isachsen Exp. in 1910.

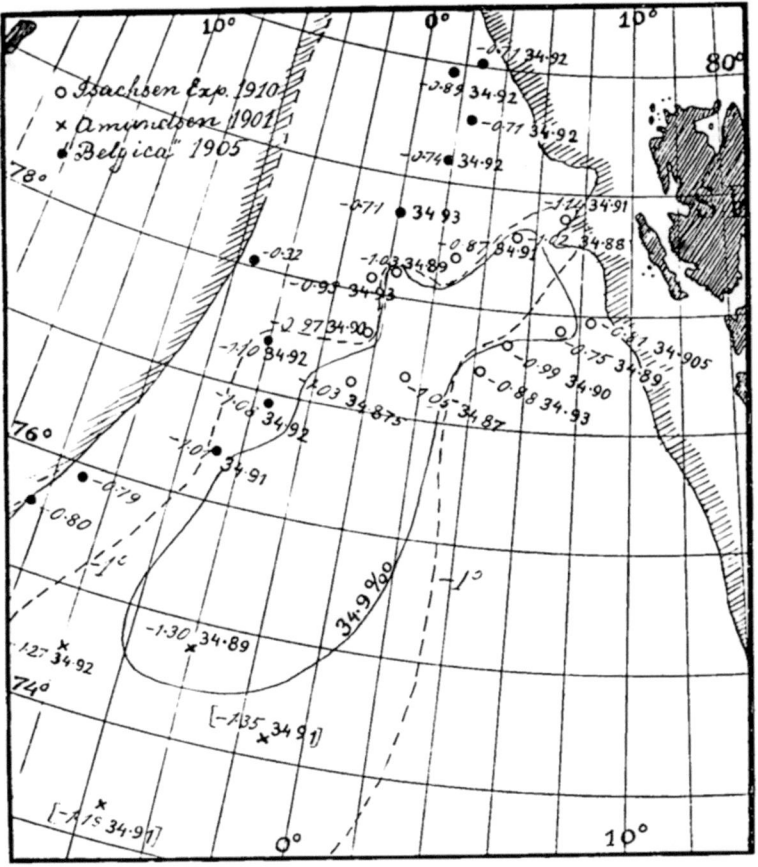

salinity of this coldest and deepest water may gradually be slightly raised. It has also to be considered that the formation of bottom-water is a somewhat complicated process going on during a great part of the winter, and that a great deal of the sinking water will not reach the greatest depths, but will form deep intermediate layers having temperatures and salinities somewhat higher than those of the coldest bottom-water.

We may thus get an explanation of the generally low salinities of the deepest and coldest water at the Isachsen stations.

Fig. 39 gives the observations in 2000 metres at the Isachsen and the Amundsen stations, and in 1800 metres at the Belgica stations. There is here a central region with salinities less than 34.90 °/oo. This may be accidental, but it may also indicate some reality. It was mentioned above that the Isachsen stations 23 and 24 were in or near the central cold area of this sea, where the cold bottom-water is formed by emission of heat from the surface during the winter. It might therefore seem probable that the bottom-water has somewhat lower salinities and also somewhat lower temperatures in this region than farther away from it. On the other hand it is also probable, according to what was mentioned above, that in 2000 metres at Isachsen's Stat. 27, near the isobath of 2000 metres on the Spitsbergen side, the salinity would be comparatively low, because this water was near the bottom. The same is also the case at the Belgica Station 16 in the north, near 80° N. Lat., where the salinities were 34.90 °/oo.

Fig. 40 gives the observations in 1200 metres, at the Isachsen and the Amundsen stations and the Belgica stations. These observations also agree fairly well in indicating a central region with low temperatures (below $-1.0°$ C.) and low salinities (below 34.90 °/oo). It therefore seems probable that this is a really existing feature, and is not merely due to errors of observation.

The Ice Fjord.

The observations at Stat. 41 (of Sept. 6, 1910) at the mouth of the Ice Fjord seem to prove that there is no high sill or threshold at the entrance of this fjord, similar to those of the deep Norwegian fjords;[1] for there is no deep layer of homogeneous water below any certain level, and the density is continually increasing with the depth. At 400 metres, near the bottom, there is a maximum of temperature (2.71° C.) as also of salinity (34.96 °/oo). This water has obviously come from the current running northwards along the coast outside the fjord. At Stats. 30 and 31 outside its entrance, water with similar temperatures and salinities occurs at 200, 220 and 240 metres (Pl. VI, Sect. IV a). At Stat. 31 the temperature was 2.73° C. and the salinity 34.965 °/oo at 220 metres on September 6th, 1910. This is practically the same; and at Stats. 31 and

---

[1] The Ice Fjord bears in its configuration more resemblance to the Finmarken fjords and the Iceland fjords than to the typical Norwegian fjords, which are compara tively narrower with deeper troughs and higher sills. [cf. Nansen 1904, p. 170]

Fig. 41. The Ice Fjord.

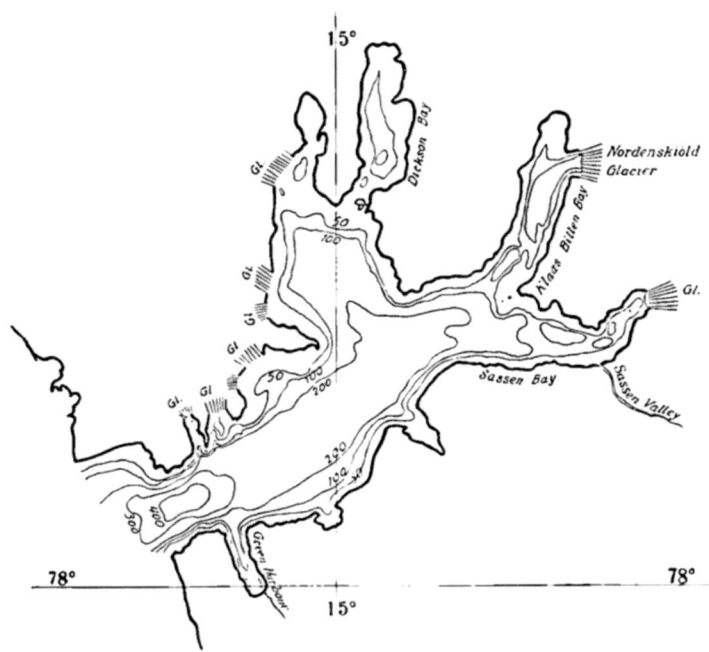

30, at 240 and 200 metres, the temperatures were 2.95° and 2.87° C. and the salinities 34.97 and 34.95 °/00 on July 23rd and 22nd, 1910. At Stat. 13 and 14, near the coast to the south, the temperatures and salinities at 150 metres were somewhat lower (2.5° C. and 2.69° C., and 34.93 °/00); and at 190 and 200 metres they were still lower. But the temperatures and the salinities were on the whole lower at these stations than at Stats. 30 and 31 to the north, probably because the influence of the cold Spitsbergen Polar Current was more appreciable in the south. To judge from the series of observations at Stat. 41, the sill, if there is one, cannot be very high, hardly higher than 300 or perhaps 250 metres; for otherwise the temperatures and salinities of the deep strata in our series would have been more uniform.

The observations at Stat. 41 (of Sept. 6, 1910) at the mouth of the Ice Fjord demonstrate a minimum of temperature of 0.52° C. in 100 metres, with a salinity of 34.50 °/00 (cf. Pl. IV, Sect. IV a).

Similar minima were observed by Dr. Johan Hjort during his visit to the Ice Fjord in the Michael Sars in July, 1901.

The following vertical series of observations were then taken:

Station	Date	Hour	Locality	Depth	t⁰ C.	S ⁰/₀₀	σ_t
87	July 26	5.30 p. m.	Green Harbour (or Green Bay)	0 m	3.8	32.11	25.53
				50 „	1.8	34.36	27.49
				100 „	0.55	.69	.86
				140 „	1.09	.79	.91
88	„	9.30 p. m.	Ice Fjord (in the middle of the fjord) off Green Harbour.	0 m	3.95	31.62	25.13
				25 „	2.03	34.17	27.33
				50 „	0.3	.38	.61
				100 „	— 0.95	.54	.80
				150 „	1.4	.79	.89
				250 „	1.42	.85	.93
89	27	3 a. m.	Mouth of Sassen Bay	0 m	3.85	31.56	25.10
				25 „	2.6	33.87	27.04
				50 „	0.7	34.27	.50
				100 „	— 1.8	.53	.82
				175 „	0.46	.79	.94
90	„	2 p. m.	In the middle of Sassen Bay, off the Sassen Valley	0 m	0.81	30.77	24.68
				25 „	1.92	33.69	26.95
				50 „	0.78	34.38	27.58
				80 „	— 0.88	.50	.76
91	„	10 p. m.	13 naut. miles West of the Ice Fjord	0 m	3.2	33.29	27.33
				25 „	2.05	34.38	.49
				50 „	1.33	.48	.62
				100 „	— 0.5	.63	.85
				150 „	1.01	.73	.86
				200 „	1.52	.88	.94

The temperature of the minima at 100 metres were there on the whole lower (—0.95⁰ and even —1.8⁰ C.) than at Stat. 41 on Sept. 6, 1910, while the salinities were nearly the same (34.54 and 34.53 ⁰/₀₀). In the inner branch of the fjord, in Sassen Bay, the minimum was — 0.88⁰ C. with a salinity of 34.50 ⁰/₀₀ in 80 metres near the bottom. Only at one station (Stat. 87), in Green Harbour, had the minimum in 100 metres approximately the same temperature (0.55⁰ C.) as at Stat. 41 of 1910; but the salinity was higher (34.69 ⁰/₀₀). At Stat. 91, in the sea outside the mouth of the Ice Fjord, there was also a low temperature-minimum of — 0.5⁰ C. in 100 metres, with a salinity of 34.63 ⁰/₀₀.

Similar minima were also observed between 60 and 100 metres at the Swedish Stations IV—VII, of July 24th and 25th, 1908, in the Ice Fjord. The temperatures of the minima were there on the whole low, even — 1.23⁰ and -1.37^0 C., while the salinity was much the same as at Stat. 41 of 1910, between 34.36 and 34.51 °/oo. Only at Stat. IV did the minimum (at 60 metres) have practically the same temperature and salinity (0.51^0 C. and 34.51^0 oo) as the minimum of Stat. 41.

According to our view, there can be no doubt that these strata, with a minimum temperature observed in the summer, are due to the vertical circulation of the upper water-strata of the fjord during the winter. We think that this is especially clearly proved by the vertical series of observations at the above-mentioned Swedish stations, which demonstrate a vertical distribution of nearly uniform salinities of about 34.4^0 oo from 20 metres down to 100 metres at Stats. V—VII. And these uniform conditions occur as late in the season as July 24th and 25th, 1908, while in September, at the Swedish Stat. III, of Sept. 1, 1908 and at our. Stat. 41 of Sept. 6, 1910 (both stations at the mouth of the Ice Fjord) they have nearly disappeared.

The process is obviously the following: By the emisssion of heat from the surface, the light surface-layers of the fjord are greatly cooled during the autumn and early winter, and much ice is formed, covering the fjord. By the growth of the ice the salinity of the surface-layers is gradually increased, and the vertical circulation caused by the cooling of the surface may thus penetrate deeper and deeper, until at the end of the winter it has reached a depth of between 60 and 100 metres, creating a layer of nearly homogeneous water between the surface and this depth, with a salinity of about 34.5^0 oo and a low temperature, both of them varying somewhat in the different parts of the fjord. In July 1901, for instance, the salinity of the temperature minimum at 100 metres in the middle of the Ice Fjord, and in Sassen Bay (Hjort's Stats. 88, 89, and 90) was between 34.50 and 34.54^0/oo, while in Green Harbour, and outside the Ice Fjord, it was between 34.60 and 34.70^0 oo at the same time, and the temperatures varied between 0.55 and -1.8^0 C.

It is obvious that where the surface-layers of the sea have comparatively low salinities at the beginning of the winter, *e. g.* in Sassen Bay, and in the Ice Fjord, the salinity of the whole homogeneous water-layer created by the vertical circulation at the end of the winter, will be comparatively low, because the underlying water with higher salinity is gradually intermixed with the overlying less saline layers, while at places where the surface-layers have higher salinities at the beginning of the winter, *e. g.* in Green Harbour and in the sea outside the Ice Fjord (Hjort's Stats. 87 and 91), the salinity of the homogeneous water-layer at the end of the winter, and of the intermediate temperature-minimum in the summer, will be higher.

This process is perfectly analogous to that by which the bottom-water of the Norwegian Sea as also that of the Barents Sea [cf. NANSEN, 1906] is formed by the cooling of the surface during the winter, only that in the Ice Fjord the vertical circulation cannot penetrate so deep, and cannot reach the bottom (except in the shallow or inner closed parts of the fjord e. g. at Hjort's Stat. 91 in Sassen Bay, cf. also the Swedish Stat. XXV in Dickson Bay) owing to the too rapid increase of salinity towards the bottom, which is due to the inflow of water along the bottom from outside.

The intermediate layer with the temperature minimum, observed in the Ice Fjord in the summer, is consequently not due to the melting of ice, as the Swedish authors believe [1911, pp. 13 et seq.], but to the cooling of the sea-surface and the formation of ice during the winter.

During the summer the surface-layers are gradually heated by the radiation of heat from the sun and their salinities are gradually much reduced by the melting of the ice, and by the river-water from land. Thus the uniform vertical distribution of temperature and salinity existing at the end of the winter, gradually disappears. There are no distinct indications of this uniformity at Hjort's stations of July, 1901; but at the Swedish stations of July, 1908, we still see traces of it in the uniform salinities, while there is very little left at Stat. III, on September 1st of that year, and at Stat. 41, on September 6th, 1910.

At the Swedish Stations VIII, of July 30th, and XXIII of Aug. 29th, 1908, in the inner part of the Ice Fjord, the heating of the upper layers was farther advanced than at Stats. V—VII nearer the mouth of the fjord, and therefore the temperature minima were situated lower, at 130 and 150 metres, but were not so cold (viz. -0.98^0 and -0.83^0 C.). In this inner region of the fjord, the cooling during the winter may have been greater, and the vertical circulation more active. This is proved by Hjort's Stat. 89 at the mouth of Sassen Bay, where 1.8° C. was observed at 100 metres on July 27th, 1901.

Traces of similar temperature minima are also perceptible in vertical series of observations taken in the sea outside the coast, on the continental shelf. It has already been pointed out that at Hjort's Stat. 91, 13 naut. miles outside the mouth of the Ice Fjord there was a minimum of -0.5^0 C. at 100 metres (with 34.63 $^0/_{00}$). At Isachsen's Stat. 31, there was a minimum of 1.05^0 C. (with 34.36 $^0/_{00}$) at 50 metres, on July 31st, 1910, and of 2.23^0 C. (with 34.62 $^0/_{00}$) at the same depth on September 6th.

At Stat. 13 there was a minimum of $1.59°$ C. at 75 metres on June 28th, and at Stat. 14 of 2.01 and $2.00°$ C. at 100 and 125 metres on the same day; but the salinities of these minima were higher — between 34.73 and 34.91 (?) $°/oo$ — at the southern stations than at Stat. 31, where they were 34.36 and $34.62 °/oo$ at 50 metres.

At the Swedish Stat. II of Aug. 30, 1908, outside the mouth of the Ice Fjord, there was also a minimum of $2.37°$ C. with a salinity of $34.65 °/oo$ at 50 metres, consequently very similar to that of Stat. 31 on Sept. 6th, 1910; while the minimum at Hjort's Stat. 91 (of July 27th, 1901) outside the mouth of the Ice Fjord was much colder ($-0.5°$ C.) and lay in 100 metres, but had a similar salinity ($34.63 °/oo$).

We consider it probable that these temperature-minima in the sea over the continental shelf, where the horizontal movement of the water is comparatively slow, are also traces of the vertical circulation during the winter. In some places the comparatively cold intermediate layers may also to some extent be due to intermixture with the water carried by the Spitsbergen Polar Current [cf. our Memoir 1909, pp. 265 *et seq.*].

Slight traces of intermediate temperature minima may also be seen in the series of observations at Isachsen's stations near the northwest coast of Spitsbergen, *e. g.* at Stat. 16 at 30 metres, and at Stat. 36 at 30 and 50 metres.

At Stats. 38, 39, and 40 on the north coast of Spitsbergen, the conditions are very peculiar. The vertical circulation has here produced a nearly uniform distribution of temperature (about $3.0°$ C.) between the surface and the bottom. At Stat. 38 the salinity is also fairly uniform about 34.3 and 34.4 $°/oo$ (very nearly the same as that of the temperature minimum in the Ice Fjord), but at Stats. 39 and 40 the value of the salinity increases more rapidly from the surface towards the bottom.

The occurrence of similar intermediate layers with temperature minima along the coasts of Spitsbergen is also proved by the observations of the Norwegian North Atlantic Expedition of 1878 and of the Nathorst Expedition of 1898, as is seen in the following table giving the observations at Mohn's Stats. 356, and 357 (which are just south of Isachsen's Stats. 30 and 31), 336, 338, 339, and 340 (which are near South Cape), and at Hamberg's Stats. G and H. The latter station is near the Spitsbergen coast south of Horn Sound, while Stat. G is far east of South Cape, towards Hope Island.

Depth M	M 356 12. VIII. 1878 78° 2′ N. 10° 19′ E.	M 357 12. VIII. 1878 78° 3′ N. 11° 18′ E.	M 336 5. VIII. 1878 76° 19′ N. 15° 42′ E.	M 338 6. VIII. 1878 76° 16′ N. 17° 40′ E.	M 339 6. VIII. 1878 76° 30′ N. 15° 39′ E.	M 340 6. VIII. 1878 70° 3′ N. 14° 40′ E.	G 24. VII. 1898 76° 40′ N. 23° 12′ E.	H 26. VII. 1898 76° 46′ N. 15° 22′ E.
0	4.4°C.	5.0°C.	1.2°C.	3.7°C.	2.6°C.	2.8°C.	2.3°C.	1.0°C.
20							1.3	−0.3
37	2.0	1.2		1.7				
50							0.2	2.5
68					0.9			
73	1.3	1.4		2.7				
100							1.3	2.9
106						0.6		
110	1.8	1.0		2.0				
128			0.4				1.7	
146	1.8	1.4		2.6				
150								2.9
165	1.2	1.2						
183	1.9	1.5		2.1				
201	2.1							
210								3.0
219				−0.1				
220		1.9						
238				−0.7				

It is also noteworthy that in the Spitsbergen Polar Current, at Amundsen's Stat. 24 (of Aug. 20, 1901) between Northeast Land and King Charles Land, a temperature minimum of − 1.94° C. with a salinity of 34.50 °/oo was observed in 60 metres [cf. NANSEN, 1906, pp. 55 and 145]. This has much similarity to the intermediate cold layer at the Swedish Stations in the Ice Fjord; but the temperature of the minimum is still lower. As the salinity near the surface at Amundsen's Stat. 24 is not very low (34.07 °/oo at 20 metres) we consider it probable that the intermediate layer with the temperature minimum is also due to the vertical circulation during the winter, which reaches to a depth of between 60 and 100 metres.

A similar vertical circulation of the water was observed during the Fram Expedition (1893—96) in the surface-layers of the North Polar Basin during the winter. But as the salinity of the surface-layers was so low, and the growth of the ice so slow (owing to its thickness), this vertical circulation did not penetrate deeper than 30 or 40 metres [cf. NANSEN, 1902, pp. 313 *et seq.*].

The Swedish oceanographers [Svenska Hydr.-Biol. Komm. 1911, pp. 10 et seq.] have given a very different explanation of the conditions in the Ice Fjord. We have already mentioned their view of the origin of the intermediate layer with a temperature minimum, which they think is due to the melting of ice. They also believe that the bottom-water of the fjord is formed in a similar manner, a view which we think is sufficiently disproved by the several vertical series of observations which they themselves have published. All these series (with the exception of a few in the innermost closed ends of the fjord) show a gradual and steady increase of the density, and with a few exceptions of the salinity also, from the surface-layers towards the bottom, which would not be possible if the bottom-water were *continually* being formed by contact of the water with ice in the upper strata. The Swedish Station IX, of August 17th, 1908, in Klaas Billen Bay, in front of the Nordenskiöld Glacier, and Stat. XXV in Dickson Bay demonstrate clearly how the vertical distribution of temperature, salinity, and density would be in a closed fjord where the bottom-water has been formed by cooling. The trough of Klaas Billen Bay is about 200 metres deep, and is separated from the basin of the Ice Fjord by a sill with a probable saddle-depth of about 60 or 70 metres. The hollow of Dickson Bay is about 100 metres deep and is separated from the Ice Fjord by a sill probably about 50 metres deep. By the cooling of the sea-surface during the winter, the water of these hollows has become nearly homogeneous as regards temperature and salinity, in the deeper strata down to the bottom, the temperatures being very low, about $-1.75°$ C. in Klaas Billen Bay and $-1.63°$ C. in Dickson Bay, and the salinities about $34.54\ ^0/_{00}$ and $34.27\ ^0/_{00}$. On August 17th and 26th, 1908, when the observations were taken, the upper strata, above the level of the sills, had acquired much higher temperatures (rising to $5.27°$ and $3.62°$ C. on the surface) and lower salinities, owing to the heating from above, the river-water from land, and the melting of the ice; but at the end of the winter there has probably been a uniform vertical distribution of temperature and salinity in these basins. The observations at Hjort's Stat. 90 (of July 20th, 1901) in Sassen Bay, indicate similar conditions. The winter-water was found at 80 metres with a temperature of $-0.88°$ C. and a salinity of $34.50\ ^0/_{00}$, while the water at 50 and 25 metres had already taken on higher temperatures.

The Swedish authors believe that the cold bottom-water in Klaas Billen Bay has been formed by the contact with the ice-wall of the Nordenskiöld Glacier. It is obvious that the contact with the glacier ice must have a cooling effect upon the sea-water, although the ice may have a higher temperature than the water; but we do not consider it probable that this cooling will be so great as the cooling due to the emission of heat from the surface and the vertical circulation thus created during the winter; and we think, that this is proved by the observations at Hjort's Stat. 89, at the mouth of Sassen Bay, and at the Swedish Stat. XXV in Dickson Bay. At the mouth of Sassen Bay, Hjort observed a temperature as low as -1.8^0 C. (with $34.53\ ^0/_{00}$) at 100 metres, although the sills of the bay inside are not so deep, and there is no glacier descending to that depth. In Dickson Bay the temperatures of the bottom water in August, 1908, were almost as low as in Klaas Billen Bay, although there is no glacier-ice to cool the waters of this fjord.

The Swedish oceanographers seem to have forgotten that a narrow coast current runs inside the Atlantic Current along the west coast of Spitsbergen, and that its waters are more or less mixed with water from the land and with the water of the Spitsbergen Polar Current coming from the east round South Cape. As we have seen, the water of the coast current has the same temperatures and salinities as the bottom-water in the outer part of the Ice Fjord, according to the observations at Isachsen's Stat. 41 as also those at Hjort's Stat. 88 and the Swedish Stats. III—VII. There is a very good agreement between all these observations[1].

The Swedish oceanographers maintain that the observations at their Stat. II of Aug. 30, 1908 (in $78^0\ 5'$ N. and $12^0\ 50'$ E. outside the mouth of the Ice Fjord), compared with those of their Stat. I (see Fig. 21 G 1), in $77^0\ 44'$ N. and 10^0 E., should prove that there is a sill between these two stations, rising to a level somewhat lower than 100 metres below the surface. We consider the existense of such a high sill to be very improbable, and that it is disproved by the vertical series of observations at the Swedish Stat. II, which has evidently been taken in the waters of the coast current, and is very similar to the series of observations taken in July and September, 1910, at Isachsen's Stats. 31 and 30, only that the Swedish salinities are on the whole higher in the surface-layers and lower in the deep layers, except at 200 metres; but the high value of $35.14\ ^0/_{00}$ found there, is obviously erroneous, as is proved by the absurd density (σ_t)

---

[1] The Swedish authors maintain that the bottom-water of the Ice Fjord should have a salinity of $34.92\ ^0/_{00}$, which is very like that of the bottom-water of the Norwegian Sea; and they base what they consider to be very important conclusions on this salinity [1911, pp. 12, 17]. Their own series of observations prove, however, that both the salinities and the temperatures of the bottom-water of the Ice Fjord vary a great deal, and it is only at one depth at one station that they have found the salinity mentioned, which is consequently accidental, as is also proved by the observations at Isachsen's Stat. 41.

of 28.03 with densities of 27.89 at 240 metres and 27.86 at 150 metres. The latter densities agree perfectly with the densities of 27.90 at 240 metres and 27.85 (and 27.87) at 150 metres at Isachsen's Stat. 31, in July and September, 1910. It is unfortunate that the Swedish authors have drawn what they consider to be important conclusions from this high value of $35.14\,^0/_{00}$ at 200 metres at their Stat. II, without noticing that it must be erroneous. The densities above and below prove that the salinity has been about $34.94\,^0/_{00}$, provided that the temperature (2.95^0 C.) observed is correct, and this salinity also agrees with the salinity of $34.95\,^0/_{00}$ (with a temperature of 2.83^0 C.) observed in 200 metres at Isachsen's Stat. 31 on September 6th, 1910. We therefore see no reason why there should be any high sill or threshold outside the Swedish Stat. II preventing the free communication of its bottom-water with the waters at the same levels of the coast current. On the contrary, we consider it probable that a submarine fjord or valley traverses the shelf from the continental slope towards the mouth of the Ice Fjord [cf. our bathymetrical chart, 1909, Pl. I].

The Swedish authors pay much attention to the melting of the ice in the Ice Fjord, which they think is chiefly due to the contact of the ice with the sea-water, and to the influx of warmer water from the Atlantic current outside the fjord. They believe that this supposed process disproves the correctness of our view that the polar ice carried by the East Greenland Polar Current is chiefly melted by the heat from above, directly due to solar radiation, during the summer, and only to a very insignificant extent by heat coming from the underlying water [1]. The Swedish authors base their argument chiefly on the conditions near a wall of glacier-ice descending to a depth of 159 metres, which is naturally a very different thing. And then they seem to have entirely forgotten that during the winter the Ice Fjord is covered with a thick layer of ice, which is formed there, and this consequently does not melt in the winter in spite of any influx of warmer water. But this ice melts during the summer, and

---

[1] Our view in this respect had led the Swedish oceanographers to the superfluous remark (1911, p. 17) that ice is melted by contact with sea-water, as long as the latter has „einen Temperaturüberschuss von einem Millionstel Grad über die Gleichgewichtstemperatur des Systems". This, however, is not the question, which is: *How much ice can be melted in this manner, e. g. in one year*, if the temperature of the sea-water be only some few tenths of a degree above its freezing point? A very simple computation will prove that, *e. g.* in the East Greenland Polar Current, it can only be quite insignificant compared with the quantity of ice which melts there every summer, as we have pointed out on several previous occasions.

the surface-layers of the fjord then acquire temperatures of as much as 4 and 5 and even 6° C. by the heating from above, and certainly not from below. If the Swedish authors were to state their case, they would at least have to prove that the melting of this ice on the surface is due to the heat of the influx of warm water by the inflowing undercurrent of the fjord, which of course is impossible.

LITERATURE.

1905. EKMAN, V. WALFRID: On the Use of Insulated Water-Bottles and Reversing Thermometers. *Publications de circonstance*, No. 23. Copenhagen, 1905.

1906. HAMBERG, AXEL: Hydrographische Arbeiten der von A. G. Nathorst geleiteten schwedischen Polarexpedition 1898. *Kungl. Svenska Vetenskaps-Akademiens Handlingar*, vol. XLI, No. 1. Stockholm, 1906.

1909. HELLAND-HANSEN, B. and KOEFOED, E.: Hydrographie. Duc d'Orléans: *Croisière océanographique 1905*. Bruxelles, 1909.

1909. HELLAND-HANSEN, B. and NANSEN, F.: The Norwegian Sea. *Report on Norwegian Fishery and Marine Investigations*, vol. II, No. 2. Bergen, 1909.

1901. MAKAROFF, S.: Yermak wo ljedakh (In the Ice). St. Petersburg, 1901 (In Russian).

1887. MOHN, H : The North Ocean, its Depths, Temperature and Circulation. *The Norwegian North-Atlantic Expedition 1876—1878*. Christiania, 1887.

1902. NANSEN, FRIDTJOF: The Oceanography of the North Polar Basin. *The Norwegian North Polar Expedition 1893—1896. Scientific Results*, vol. III, No. 9. Christiania.

1904. NANSEN, F.: The Bathymetrical Features of the North Polar Seas, etc. *Norw. N. Polar Exp. 1803—1896. Scient. Res.* vol. IV, No. 13. Christiania.

1906. NANSEN, F.: Northern Waters. *Videnskabs-Selskabets Skrifter 1906. I. Math.-naturv. Kl.*, No. 3. Christiania, 1906.

1907. D'ORLEANS, DUC: Croisière Océanographique accomplie à bord de la Belgica dans la Mer du Grönland 1905. Bruxelles, 1907.

1898. PETTERSSON, O. and EKMAN, G. (unter Mitwirkung von P. T. CLEVE): Die Hydrographischen Verhältnisse der oberen Wasserschichten des nördlichen Nordmeeres zwischen Spitsbergen, Grönland und der Norwegischen Küste in den Jahren 1896 und 1897. *Bihang till K. Svenska Vet.-Akad. Handlingar*, vol. XXIII, Part II, No. 4. Stockholm, 1898.

1911. Svenska Hydrografisk-Biologiska Kommissionen: Hydrographische Beobachtungen; *Zoologische Ergebnisse der schwedischen Expedition nach Spitzbergen 1908 unter Leitung von Prof. G. de Geer*. Part I, No. 1. *Kungl. Svenska Vetenskaps-Akademiens Handlingar*, vol. XLV, No. 9. Stockholm, 1911.

TABLE I

gives the vertical series of observations at the Stations, taken between June and September 1910.

The heading for each Station gives: the Number of the Station, the Date, the Hours (in parenthesis), the Latitude and Longitude, the Depth of the sea (and Nature of Bottom in parenthesis), the Temperature of the Air, and the Observer (G. I. = Captain GUNNAR ISACHSEN; A. H. = Captain A. HERMANSEN; P.-H. = Captain PETTERSEN-HANSEN).

1st Column. Depth in Metres.

2nd Column. Instrument used. **B.** = Bucket used for surface-water; the temperature was then taken with an ordinary thermometer inserted in the water of the bucket. **P.-N.** = the Pettersson-Nansen Insulated Water-Bottle; the Nansen Thermometer No. 952 (PTR. 37344) was always used with this instrument. **P.** = the Pettersson Insulated Water-Bottle of the old model, used with the Nansen Thermometer No. 952. **E.** = the Ekman Reversing Water-Bottle with the Richter Reversing Thermometer No. 60.

3rd Column, t^0 C. The corrected Temperature (Centigrade) *in situ*. The temperatures in parenthesis at Stations 1—14 are the readings of the Nansen Thermometer No. 952, only corrected for the adiabatic effect by change of pressure, but not for instrumental error.

4th Column, $S^0/_{00}$. Salinity.

5th Column, σ_t. Density (i. e. $(S_0^t - 1) \cdot 1000$) at the temperature *in situ* and at the pressure of one atmosphere.

Depth Metres	Instrument	t^0 C.	$S^0/_{00}$	σ_t
\multicolumn{5}{c}{Stat. 1. 25. VI. 1910 (5.45—6.45 a. m.)}
\multicolumn{5}{c}{74° 40' N., 16° 10' E. 330 m. Air $t^0 = 0.5^0$ C. Obs. A. H.}
0	B.	4.03	34.91	27.74
20	P. N.	4.08 (3.28)	34.85	27.68
50	»	4.93 (4.13)	35.01	27.71
75	»	4.88 (4.08)	35.06	27.76
100	»	4.36 (3.56)	35.00	27.77
200	»	4.19 (3.39)	35.07	27.85
300	E.	3.37	35.06	27.93
\multicolumn{5}{c}{Stat. 2. 25. VI. 1910 (9.35—10.25 a. m.)}
\multicolumn{5}{c}{74° 52' N., 15° 5' E. Air $t^0 = 0.7^0$ C. Obs. P.-H.}
0	B.	5.38	35.08	27.72
20	P. N.	5.48 (4.08)	35.08	27.71
50	»	4.52 (3.72)	35.04	27.78
75	»	4.31 (3.51)	35.075	27.84
100	»	4.27 (3.47)	35.06	27.82
200	»	3.52 (2.72)	35.05	27.99
400	E.	2.32	35.05	28.02
600	»		34.94	
\multicolumn{5}{c}{Stat. 3. 25. VI. 1910 (1.40—2.30 p. m.)}
\multicolumn{5}{c}{74° 55' N., 13° 40' E. Air $t^0 = 1.2^0$ C. Obs. P.-H.}
0	B.	4.83	35.03	27.74
20	P. N.	4.68 (3.88)	35.06	27.78
50	»	4.19 (3.39)	35.04	27.83
75	»	4.07 (3.27)	35.02	27.82
100	»	3.87 (3.07)	35.06	27.87
200	»	3.20 (2.40)	35.02	27.92
400	»	2.25 (1.45)	35.00	27.98
500	E.	1.04	34.98	27.99
600	»	1.00	34.91	28.00

Depth Metres	Instrument	t° C.	$S^0/_{00}$	σ_t
\multicolumn{5}{c}{**Stat. 4.** 25. VI. 1910 (8—8.40 p. m.)}				
\multicolumn{5}{c}{75° 8' N., 11° 20' E. Air $t^0 = 2.2^\circ$ C. Obs. A. H.}				
0	B.	4.49	35.00	27.83
20	P.-N.	4.37 (3.57)	35.08	27.83
50	"	3.96 (3.16)	35.06	27.86
75	"	3.89 (3.09)	35.01	27.83
100	"	3.79 (2.99)	35.04	27.87
200	"	3.26 (2.46)	35.05	27.93
400	E.	2.59	34.98	27.94
600	"	1.67	34.94	27.98
\multicolumn{5}{c}{**Stat. 5.** 26. VI. 1910 (5—5.45 a. m.)}				
\multicolumn{5}{c}{75° 27'.5 N., 7° 40' E. Air $t^0 = 1.5^\circ$ C. Obs. P.-H.}				
0	B.	3.93	35.05	27.86
20	P.-N.	3.90 (3.10)	35.02	27.84
50	"	3.65 (2.85)	35.04	27.89
75	"	3.59 (2.79)	35.05	27.90
100	"	3.51 (2.71)	35.06	27.91
200	"	3.27 (2.47)	35.06	27.94
400	E.	2.85	35.01	27.94
500	"	1.73	35.05 (?)	28.06 (?)
600	"	1.38	34.97	28.02
\multicolumn{5}{c}{**Stat. 6.** 26. VI. 1910 (1.30—4.30 p. m.)}				
\multicolumn{5}{c}{75° 45' N., 4° 20' E. Air $t^0 = 4.5^\circ$ C. Obs. A. H. and P.-H.}				
0	B.	4.18	34.97	27.77
20	P.-N.	3.76 (2.96)	34.98	27.82
50	"	2.86 (2.06)	34.94	27.88
75	"	1.91 (1.11)	34.93	27.96
100	"	1.37 (0.57)	34.88	27.95
150	"	0.64 (—0.16)	34.88	28.00
200	"	—0.30 (—1.10)	34.84	28.03
300	"	—0.28 (—1.08)	34.80	28.06
400	"	—0.39 (—1.19)	34.85	28.04
500	"	—0.50 (—1.36)	34.89	28.07
600	E.	—0.82	34.89	28.08
800	"	—0.00	34.95	28.13

Depth Metres	Instrument	t^0 C.	$S\,^0/_{00}$	σ_t
	Stat. 7. 27. VI. 1910 (3.15—4 a. m.) 75° 57' N., 7° 30' E. Air $t^0 = 3.5^0$ C. Obs. P.-H.
0	B.	4.43	35.08	27.83
20	P.-N.	4.08 (3.28)	35.03	27.83
50	"	3.55 (2.75)	35.08	27.93
75	"	3.56 (2.76)	35.08	27.93
100	"	3.49 (2.69)	35.01 (?)	27.88 (?)
200	"	3.08 (2.28)	35.02	27.93
400	E.	2.27	35.04	28.01
600	"		34.94	
	Stat. 8. 27. VI. 1910 (10—10.30 a. m.) 76° 6' N., 9° 45' E. Air $t^0 = 3.5^0$ C. Obs. A. H.
0	B.	4.39	34.97	27.75
20	P.-N.	5.10 (4.30)	34.95	27.65
50	"	3.69 (2.89)	34.98	27.83
75	"	3.54 (2.74)	34.99	27.85
100	"	3.06 (2.26)	35.03	27.94
200	"	2.82 (2.02)	35.04	27.97
400	"	2.02 (1.22)	34.98	27.98
600	E.	0.88	34.88	27.99
	Stat. 9. 27. VI. 1910 (2.40—3.10 p. m.) 76° 11' N., 11° 15' E. Air $t^0 = 3.5^0$ C. Obs. A. H.
0	B.	4.23	34.54	27.42
20	P.-N.	4.39 (3.59)	34.94	27.72
50	"	4.35 (3.55)	34.97	27.75
75	"	4.09 (3.29)	35.05 (?)	27.84 (?)
100	"	4.05 (3.25)	34.99	27.80
200	"	3.23 (2.43)	34.96	27.86
400	E.	2.29	34.99	27.97
600	"	1.15	34.96	28.04

Depth Metres	Instrument	t^0 C.	$S^0/_{00}$	σ_t

Stat. 10. 27. VI. 1910 (6.30—7 p. m.)
76^0 16' N., 12^0 30' E. Air $t^0 = 1.5^0$ C. Obs. A. H.

Depth Metres	Instrument	t^0 C.	$S^0/_{00}$	σ_t
0	B.	4.32	34.70	27.01
20	P.-N.	4.29 (3.49)	34.80	27.07
50	»	4.40 (3.00)	34.90	27.76
75	»	4.39 (3.59)	35.05	27.81
100	»	3.86 (3.06)	34.06 (?)	27.79 (?)
200	»	3.23 (2.43)	35.06	27.94
300	»	2.60 (1.80)	34.99	27.95
400	E.	2.09	34.00	27.97
600	»	0.45	34.99	28.10

Stat. 11. 27. VI. 1910 (10—10.45 p. m.)
76^0 20' N., 13^0 45' E. Air $t^0 = -0.5^0$ C. Obs. G. I. and P.-H.

Depth Metres	Instrument	t^0 C.	$S^0/_{00}$	σ_t
0	B.	4.63	34.70	27.50
20	P.-N.	5.35 (4.55)	34.90	27.02
50	»	3.90 (3.10)	34.88	27.73
75	«	4.58 (3.78)	35.00	27.79
100	»	4.55 (3.75)	35.04	27.78
200	»	3.86 (3.00)	35.05	27.87
300	»	3.37 (2.57)	35.05	27.92
400	E.	2.62	35.04	27.98
600	»	1.84	34.07	27.99

Stat. 12. 28. VI. 1910 (5.45—6.15 a. m.)
76^0 56' N., 11^0 0' E. Air $t^0 = 5.8^0$ C. Obs. G. I. and P.-H.

Depth Metres	Instrument	t^0 C.	$S^0/_{00}$	σ_t
0	B.	4.20	33.92	26.93
20	P.-N.	4.00 (3.20)	34.94	27.77
50	»	3.97 (3.17)	34.99	27.81
75	»	3.69 (2.89)	34.97	27.82
100	»	3.60 (2.80)	34.95	27.81
200	»	2.82 (2.02)	35.00	27.93
400	E.	2.00	35.08 (?)	28.00 (?)
600	»	0.94	34.04	28.03

Depth Metres	Instrument	t^0 C.	$S^0/_{00}$	σ_t
\multicolumn{5}{c}{Stat. 13. 28. VI. 1910 (8.30—9 a. m.)}
\multicolumn{5}{c}{77^0 2′ N., 12^0 21′ E. 208 m. (Clay). Air $t^0 = 4.3^0$ C. Obs. G. I. and P.-H}
0	B.	3.39	33.35	26.56
20	P.-N.	2.52 (1.72)	34.38	27.46
50	»	2.08 (1.28)	34.64	27.70
75	»	1.59 (0.79)	34.73	27.82
100	»	2.24 (1.44)	34.87	27.88
150	»	2.50 (1.70)	34.93	27.91
190	E.	2.10	34.91	27.93
\multicolumn{5}{c}{Stat. 14. 28. VI. 1910 (10.30—12 a. m.)}
\multicolumn{5}{c}{77^0 10′ N., 13^0 5′ E. 213 m. (Clay). Air $t^0 = 7.0^0$ C. Obs. G. I. and A. H.}
0	B.	3.32	33.95	27.04
5	P.-N.	2.89 (2.09)	34.00	27.12
10	»	2.70 (1.90)	34.03	27.16
20	»	2.05 (1.25)	34.22	27.36
30	»	2.18 (1.38)	34.47	27.56
40	»	2.65 (1.85)	34.61	27.62
50	»	2.79 (1.99)	34.72	27.71
75	»	2.58 (1.78)	34.81	27.80
100	»	2.01 (1.21)	34.91 (?)	27.93 (?)
125	»	2.00 (1.20)	34.91 (?)	27.93 (?)
150	»	2.69 (1.89)	34.93	27.89
175	»	2.50 (1.70)	34.91	27.88
200	»	2.00 (1.20)	34.86	27.88
\multicolumn{5}{c}{Stat. 15. 17. VII. 1910 (10.30—10.45 a. m.)}
\multicolumn{5}{c}{79^0 10′ N., 10^0 30′ E. 39 m. (Rock). Air $t^0 = 4.0^0$ C. Obs. P.-H.}
0	B.	0.49	33.79	26.56
10	P.-N.	0.31	33.78	20.58
20	»	3.81	33.07	27.01
30	»	1.01	34.17	27.36

Depth Metres	Instrument	t^0 C.	S^0_{00}	σ_t
	Stat. 16. 17. VII. 1910 (1.45—2.40 p. m.) 79° 17' N., 8° 57' E. 213 m. (Clay). Air $t^0 = 5.0°$ C. Obs. P.-H.			
0	B.	0.23	34.20	26.01
10	P.-N.	6.38	34.26	26.94
20	»	4.08	34.55	27.44
30	»	3.37	34.81	27.73
50	»	3.68	34.87	27.74
75	»	4.09	34.96	27.77
100	»	3.79	34.94	27.79
150	»	2.93	34.92	27.86
200	»	2.77	34.00	27.86
	Stat. 17. 17. VII. 1910 (6.0—8.15 p. m.) 78° 53' N., 7° 20' E. 1210 m. (Sand and Clay). Air $t^0 = 5.8°$ C. Obs. P.-H.			
0	B.	6.03	34.17	26.91
10	P.-N.	6.48	34.12	26.81
20	»	5.05	34.81	27.55
30	»	4.81	34.93	27.66
50	»	4.51	34.98	27.74
75	»	4.34	34.97	27.75
100	»	3.99	34.98	27.80
150	»	3.56	34.96	27.83
200	»	3.55	34.96	27.83
300	»	2.50	34.95	27.91
400	»	2.40	34.99	27.96
500	»	2.11	34.97	27.97
600	E.	1.70	34.97	28.00
800	»	0.51	34.96	28.08
1200	»	—1.14	34.91	28.11

Depth Metres	Instrument	t^0 C.	$S^0/_{00}$	σ_t

Stat. 18. 18. VII. 1910 (0.45—2.15 a. m.)

78^0 40' N., 5^0 2' E. $\frac{-}{1640}$ m. Air $t^0 = 4.5^0$ C. Obs. P.-H.

Depth Metres	Instrument	t^0 C.	$S^0/_{00}$	σ_t
0	B.	6.43	34.76	27.34
10	P.-N.	6.53	34.74	27.31
20	»	5.85	34.95	27.50
30	»	4.93	34.94	27.66
50	»	3.51	34.97	27.84
75	»	3.06	34.97	27.89
100	»	2.96	35.00	27.92
150	»	2.34	34.95	27.94
200	»	2.05	34.95	27.96
300	»	1.70	34.95	27.99
400	»	1.20	34.91	27.99
500	»	0.11	34.86	28.02
600	E.	— 0.42	34.90	28.07
800	»	— 0.59	34.87	28.05
1200	»	— 1.02	34.88	28.07

Stat. 19. 18. VII. 1910 (7.30—8.45 a. m.)

78^0 27' N., 2^0 43' E. $_{1640}$ m. Air $t^0 = 4.2^0$ C. Obs. P.-H.

Depth Metres	Instrument	t^0 C.	$S^0/_{00}$	σ_t
0	B.	6.08	34.95	27.53
10	P.-N.	5.85	34.95	27.56
20	»	5.23	34.98	27.60
30	»	4.11	34.97	27.78
50	»	3.45	35.00	27.88
75	»	3.24	35.04	27.93
100	»	3.09	35.00	27.91
150	»	3.04	35.01	27.92
200	»	2.45	35.00	27.97
300	»	2.20	34.99	27.98
400	»	1.85	34.99	28.01
500	»	1.01	34.95	28.04
600	E.	0.02	34.88	28.03
800	»	—0.01	34.89	28.07
1200	»	—0.87	34.91	28.10

Depth Metres	Instrument	t^0 C.	$S°/_{00}$	σ_t

Stat. 20. 18. VII. 1910 (2.0 – 4.0 p. m.)
88° 13'.5 N., 0° 24' E. $\frac{-}{1640}$ m. Air $t^0 = 3.0°$ C. Obs. P.-H.

Depth Metres	Instrument	t^0 C.	$S°/_{00}$	σ_t
0	B.	4.43	33.67	26.74
10	P.-N.	4.11	33.73	26.80
20	"	2.19	34.68	27.72
30	"	2.11	34.83	27.86
50	"	2.13	34.90	27.91
75	"	2.19	34.91	27.91
100	"	1.97	34.96	27.97
150	"	1.76	34.92	27.96
200	"	1.63	34.93	27.98
300	"	0.85	34.95	28.05
400	"	0.15	34.89	28.04
500	E.	−0.00	34.90	28.08
600	"	−0.07	34.90	28.08
800	"	−0.84	34.88	28.07
1200	"	−1.03	34.89	28.09
1500	"	−1.08	34.92	28.11

Stat. 21. 18. VII. 1910 (6.30 – 10.30 p. m.)
78° 8' N., 0° 35' W. At the ice-edge. Air $t^0 = 0.5°$ C. Obs. P.-H.

Depth Metres	Instrument	t^0 C.	$S°/_{00}$	σ_t
0	B.	2.73	33.36	26.62
10	P.-N.	2.34	33.91	27.12
20	"	2.95	34.73	27.70
30	"	2.79	34.93	27.88
50	"	2.55	34.97	27.94
75	"	2.19	34.90	27.91
100	"	2.03	34.97	27.98
150	"	1.07	34.95	27.99
200	"	1.54	34.95	28.00
300	"	1.00	35.00	28.08
400	"	0.11	34.90	28.05
500	"	−0.29	34.88	28.04
600	E.	−0.38	34.97 (?)	28.12 (?)
800	"	−0.57	34.92	28.09
1200	"	−0.93	{34.93 / 34.93}	28.11
1500	"	1.01	{34.88 / 34.88}	28.08
2000	"	−1.19	{34.88 / 34.88}	28.08

Depth Metres	Instrument	t^0 C.	$S^0/_{00}$	σ_t
Stat. 22. 19. VII. 1910 (2.15—5.45 p. m.) 77° 41′ N., 0° 22′ W. At the ice-edge. Air $t^0 = 5.5^0$ C. Obs. P.-H.				
0	B.	4.38	33.71	26.74
10	P.-N.	4.42	34.14	27.08
20	»	3.08	34.75	27.70
30	»	2.63	34.93	27.89
50	»	2.48	34.97	27.94
75	»	2.38	34.97	27.95
100	»	2.00	34.96	27.97
150	»	1.90	34.96	27.98
200	»	0.01	34.95	28.06
300	»	0.60	34.89	28.01
400	»	−0.10	34.88	28.04
500	»	−0.46	34.86	28.04
600	E.	−0.05	34.88	28.06
800	»	−0.76	{ 34.92 { 34.02	28.10
1200	»	−0.97	{ 34.00 { 34.90	28.09
1500	»	−1.00	{ 34.80 { 34.91	28.09 28.10
2000	»	−1.15	{ 34.88 { 34.80	28.08 28.00
Stat. 23. 19. VII. 1910 (9.30 p. m.—0.30 a. m. 20 VII) 77° 15′ N., 0° 35′ W. Air $t^0 = 4.6^0$ C. Obs. P.-H.				
0	B.	4.08	33.02	26.04
10	P.-N.	4.08	34.14	27.12
20	»	3.93	34.60	27.58
40	»	0.78	34.72	27.86
50	»	0.28	34.78	27.94
75	»	−0.01	34.81	27.08
100	»	−0.21	34.82	28.00
150	»	−0.57	34.80	28.07
200	»	−0.67	34.89	28.07
300	»	−0.90	34.85	28.05
400	»	−0.83	34.01	28.09
500	»	−0.96	34.80	28.00
600	E.	−0.83		
800	»	−0.92	{ 34.92 { 34.92	28.11
1200	»	1.03	{ 34.88 { 34.87	28.07
1500	»	−1.10	[34.05]	
2000	»	−1.22	{ 34.88 { 34.90	28.08 28.10

Depth Metres	Instrument	$t°$ C.	$S°/_{00}$	σ_t
	Stat. 24. 20. VII. 1910 (8.45 a. m.—0.30 p. m.) 77° 22' N., 1° 23' E. Air $t°$ = 3.7° C. Obs. P.-H.				
0	B.	4.08	34.52	27.41
10	P.-N.	3.22	34.54	27.52
20	»	3 03	34.67	27.65
30	»	1.43	34.82	27.90
50	»	0.73	34.79	27.92
75	»	—0.11	34.88	28.03
100	»	—0.14	34.82	28.00
150	»	—0.38	34.87	28.04
200	»	—0.75	34.82	28.03
300	»	—0.74	34.86	28.05
400	»	—0.80	34.85	28.04
500	»	—0.82	84.84	28.04
600	E.	—0.78	34.86	28.05
800	»	—0.93	{ 34.92 / 34.92	28.11
1200	»	—1.05	{ 34.87 / 34.87	28 07
1500	»	—1.14	{ 34.89 / 34.91	28.09 / 28.10
2000	»	—1.24	{ 34.90 / 34.88	28.10 / 28.09
	Stat. 25. 20. VII. 1910 (6.30—10.0 p. m.) 77° 29' N., 4° 11' E. Air $t°$ = 5.7° C. Obs. P.-H.				
0	B.	5.08	34.94	27.57
10	P.-N.	5.67	34.95	27.58
20	»	4.28	34.93	27.73
30	»	3.91	34.97	27.80
50	»	3.48	34 97	27.85
75	»	3.42	35.00	27.88
100	»	3.22	35.00	27.90
150	»	2.70	34.99	27.93
200	»	2.55	35.03	27.98
300	»	2.25	34.99	27.97
400	»	1.01	34.95	27.97
500	»	1.25	34.93	28.00
600	E.	0.27	34.89	28.03
800	»	—0.51	{ 34.88 / 34.90	28.06 / 28 07
1200	»	—0 88	{ 34 94 / 34.92	28.12 / 28.10
1500	»	—1.06	{ 34.92 / 34.92	28.11
2000	»	—1.17	{ 34 92 / 34.92	28.11

Depth Metres	Instrument	t^0 C.	$S^0/_{00}$	σ_t
	Stat. 26. 22. VII. 1910 (2.15—5.45 a. m.) $77^0 43'$ N., $5^0 15'$ E. Air $t^0 = 7.0^0$ C. Obs. P.-H.			
0	B.	5.68	34.88	27.53
10	P.-N.	5.53	34.89	27.55
20	»	5.53	34.88	27.54
30	»	5.34	34.89	27.57
50	»	4.13	34.93	27.74
75	»	3.76	35.03	27.86
100	»	3.54	35.02	27.88
150	»	3.25	35.00	27.00
200	»	2.75	35.01	27.95
300	»	2.15	34.94	27.94
400	»	1.58	34.96	28.01
500	»	0.01	34.92	28.02
600	E.	−0.14	34.84 (?)	28.01 (?)
800	»	−0.59	{ 34.92 / 34.94	28.09 / 28.11
1200	»	−0.99	{ 34.90 / 34.90	28.09
2000	»	−1.26	{ 34.90 / 34.92	28.10 / 28.12
	Stat. 27. 22. VII. 1910 (11.0 a. m.—2.15 p. m.) $77^0 53'$ N., $7^0 21'$ E. Air $t^0 = 9.5^0$ C. Obs. P.-H.			
0	B.	6.23	34.88	27.46
10	P.-N.	5.92	34.88	27.49
20	»	5.77	34.88	27.51
30	»	4.67	34.96	27.71
50	»	4.18	34.98	27.78
75	»	3.92	34.99	27.81
100	»	3.72	35.00	27.84
150	»	3.33	35.02	27.90
200	»	3.05	35.01	27.92
300	»	2.47	35.00	27.96
400	»	2.21	35.02 (?)	28.00 (?)
500	»	2.05	34.99	27.99
600	E.	1.76	34.97	28.00
800	»	−0.12	{ 34.91 / 34.89	28.06 / 28.04
1200	»	−0.75	{ 34.90 / 34.88	28.08 / 28.07
1500	»	−0.92	{ 34.88 / 34.88	28.10
2000	»	−1.28	{ 34.88 / 34.90	28.09 / 28.10

Depth Metres	Instrument	t^0 C.	$S^0{}_{(0)}$	σ_t
Stat. 28 22. VII. 1910 (3.45—5.45 p. m.)				
77° 57′ N., 8° 32′ E. 1640 m. Air $t^0 = 8.8^0$ C. Obs. P.-H.				
0	B	6.00	34.98	27.44
10	P. N.	6.28	34.83	27.41
20	»	6.18	34.83	27.42
30	»	4.73	35.00	27.73
50	»	4.43	35.02	27.78
75	»	4.14	35.01	27.81
100	»	3.66	35.03	27.88
150	»	3.23	34.99	27.89
200	»	3.15	35.01	27.91
300	»	2.46	34.96	27.94
400	»	2.42	34.98	27.95
500	»	1.98	34.94	27.96
600	E.	1.27	34.96	28.03
800	»	−0.22	{ 34.87 / 34.87₅	28.03 / 28.04
1200	»	−0.81	{ 34.90 / 34.91	28.08 / 28.09
1500	»	−1.05	{ 34.91 / 34.91	28.10
Stat. 29. 22. VII. 1910 (6.45—8.25 p. m.)				
78° 1′ N., 9° 10′ E. 1075 m. (Brown Clay). Air $t^0 = 7.2^0$ C. Obs. P.-H.				
0	B	6.03	34.79	27.29
10	P.-N.	6.15	34.70	27.37
20	»	6.07	34.77	27.39
30	»	4.26	34.98	27.77
50	»	4.02	34.96	27.78
75	»	3.06	34.99	27.84
100	»	3.48	35.01	27.88
150	»	2.93	35.00	27.93
200	»	2.84	35.00	27.93
300	»	2.35	35.00	27.98
400	»	2.16	35.01	28.00
500	»	2.02	34.97	27.98
600	E.	1.03	34.90	28.07
800	»	−0.09	{ 34.88 / 34.89	28.03 / 28.04
1000	»	−0.99	{ 34.89 / 34.91	28.08 / 28.10

Depth Metres	Instrument	t^0 C.	$S^0/_{00}$	σ_t

Stat. 30. 22. VII. 1910 (10.0—10.40 p. m.)
78^0 5' N., 10^0 0' E. 235 m. (Rock). Air $t^0 = 7.5^0$ C. Obs. P.-H.

Depth Metres	Instrument	t^0 C.	$S^0/_{00}$	σ_t
0	B.	6.43	34.73	27.31
10	P.-N.	5.95	34.72	27.37
20	»	5.87	34.72	27.38
30	»	5.02	34.70	27.39
50	»	4.13	34.54	27.43
75	»	3.85	34.97	27.80
100	»	3.65	34.94	27.80
150	»	3.34	34.90	27.88
200	»	2.87	34.95	27.89

Stat. 31. 23. VII 1910. (0.15—1.15 a. m.)
78^0 3' N., 11^0 0' E. 255 m. (Brown Clay). Air $t^0 = 6.5^0$ C. Obs. P.-H.

Depth Metres	Instrument	t^0 C.	$S^0/_{00}$	σ_t
0	B.	5.18	32.84	25.07
10	P.-N.	5.14	33.42	26.44
20	»	5.11	33.88	26.80
30	»	3.55	34.14	27.17
50	»	1.05	24.36	27.55
75	»	2.53	34.70	27.71
100	»	2.02	34.76	27.81
150	»	3.49	34.98	27.85
200	»	3.15	35.01	27.91
240	»	2.95	34.97	27.90

Stat. 32. 8. VIII. 1910 (10.0 p. m. 8 VIII—1.0 a. m. 9 VIII)
Bock Bay.[1] 78 m. Air $t^0 = 5.7^0$ C. Obs. G. J. and P.-H.

Depth Metres	Instrument	t^0 C.	$S^0/_{00}$	σ_t
0	B.	5.33		
5	P ?	5.28		
»	E.	2.49	17.24	13.81
10	P. (E)	1.73	18.47	14.81
20	» »	2.70	18.83	15.07
30	» »	3.35	18.03	15.11
40	» »	3.20	18.93	15.12
50	» »	2.03	18.91	15.10
60	» »	1.18	18.91	15.18
70	» »	0.60	18.93	15.19

On the shore just inside this station a spring was coming up from the soil, the water of which had a temperature of 24.2^0 C.

The Richter reversing thermometer No. 60 was used with the Ekman reversing waterbottle when the water-samples were taken; but the thermometer gave absurd readings (e. g. -2.45^0, -3.11^0 etcs.). A new series of temperatures were taken with similar results. The temperatures were then taken with the old Pettersson insulated waterbottle (as given above).

Depth Metres	Instrument	t^0 C.	$S^0/_{00}$	σ

Stat. 33. 19. VIII. 1910 (2.10—3.30 a. m.)
79° 44' N., 10° 25' E. 120 m. (Rock). Air $t^0 = -0.2°$ C. Obs. P.-H.

Depth Metres	Instrument	t^0 C.	$S^0/_{00}$	σ
0	B.	3.49	33.89	26.97
10	P.	3.48	33.95	27.02
20	»	3.08	34.52	27.51
30	»	2.63	34.03	27.64
50	»	3.41	34.90 (?)	27.79 (?)
60	»	3.03	34.69	27.66
75	»	2.89	34.84	27.80
100	»	3.04	34.93	27.86

Stat. 34. 10. VIII. 1910 (5.15—6.45 a. m.)
79° 51'5 N., 9° 45' E. 425 m. (Clay). Air $t^0 = -1.0°$ C. Obs. A.-H.

Depth Metres	Instrument	t^0 C.	$S^0/_{00}$	σ
0	B.	2.93	33.62	26.81
10	P.	2.89	33.62	26.82
20	»	5.13	34.51	27.29
»	»	4.93	34.71	27.48
30	»	4.52	34.78	27.58
50	»	3.95	(35.11)	
75	»	3.24	34.95	27.85
100	»	3.16	35.00	27.90
150	»	2.86	34.99	27.93
200	E.	[3.15]	34.97	
300	»	[3.21]	34.96	
400	»	[3.11]	34.97	

Stat. 35. 19. VIII. 1910 (8.30—9.45 a. m.)
80° 0' N., 8° 55' E. 490 m. (Clay). Air $t^0 = 0.0°$ C. Obs. P.-H.

Depth Metres	Instrument	t^0 C.	$S^0/_{00}$	σ
0	B.	1.38	32.91	26.36
10	P.	1.72	32.95	26.38
20	»	5.25	34.54	27.30
30	»	5.08	34.84	27.56
50	»	3.58	34.88	27.76
75	»	3.46	34.95	27.83
100	»	3.55	34.97	27.84
150	»	3.14	[34.58]	
200	»	3.13	34.97	27.87
300	E.	2.39	34.82 (?)	27.82 (?)
400	»	2.05	[34.36]	
450	»	1.95	35.00	28.01

Depth Metres	Instrument	t^0 C.	$S\,{}^0/_{00}$	σ_t
Stat. 36. 19. VIII. 1910 (1.50—2.30 p. m.)				
79° 29′ N., 9° 30′ E. 125 m. (Rock). Air $t^0 = 1.0^0$ C. Obs. P.-H.				
0	B.	4.48	33.70	26.72
10	P.	4.51	33.73	26.72
20	»	3.58	34.30	27.34
30	»	2.05	34.58	27.60
50	»	2.84	34.81	27.78
75	»	3.28	34.97	27.86
100	»	2.62	35.00	27.95
Stat. 37. 19. VIII. 1910 (4.30—6.0 p. m.)				
79° 33′ N., 8° 10′ E. 823 m. (Gravel). Air $t^0 = 3.5^0$ C. Obs. A.-H.				
0	B.	3.04	33.50	26.70
10	P.	3.88	33.77	26.84
20	»	4.52	33.78	26.86
30	»	5.41	34.70	27.41
50	»	3.74	34.91	27.77
75	»	3.80	35.00	27.83
100	»	3.34	34.94	27.83
150	»	3.22	35.00	27.90
200	»	3.60	35.02	27.94
300	»	2.56	35.00	27.00
400	E.	[3.13]	35.00	
500	»	[3.31]	34.96	
600	»	[3.44]	34.97	
800	»	[3.27]	34.89	
Stat. 38. 26. VIII. 1910 (3.15—4.0 p. m.)				
79° 56′ N., 12° 5′ E. 72 and 87 m. (Rock). Air $t^0 = 0.8^0$ C. Obs. P.-H.				
0	B.	3.20	34.31	27.34
10	P. N.	3.13	34.30	27.34
20	»	3.08	34.34	27.37
30	»	3.08	34.35	27.38
40	»	3.08	34.39	27.41
50	»	3.01	34.43	27.45
60	»	3.04	34.42	27.44

Depth Metres	Instrument	t^0 C.	$S\ ^0/_{00}$	σ
Stat. 39. 26. VIII. 1910 (5.0—5.40 p. m.) 80° 1' N., 12° 5' E. 100 and 82 m. (Rock). Air $t^0 = 0.5°$ C. Obs. P.-H.				
0	B.	3.03	34.24	27.30
10	P.-N.	3.04	34.35	27.39
20	»	3.03	34.42	27.44
30	»	3.03	34.56	27.55
40	»	3.03	34.59	27.58
50	»	3.01	34.81	27.76
60	»	3.00	34.86	27.80
70	»	2.96	34.86	27.81
80	»	2.98	34.87	27.81
Stat. 40 26. VIII. 1910 (6.30—7.0 p. m.) 80°10' N., 12° 4' E. At the Ice-edge. 75 and 68 m. (Sand). Air $t^0 = 0.8°$ C. Obs. P.-H.				
0	B.	2.88	34.16	27.25
10	P.-N.	2.93	34.30	27.35
20	»	2.91	34.61	27.61
30	»	2.87	34.79	27.76
40	»	2.89	34.86	27.81
50	»	2.91	34.85	27.80
60	»	2.91	34.88	27.83
65	»	2.91	34.87	27.82
Stat 41 6 IX — 1910 (1.15 —2.30 a. m.) The Svensksund Deep (mouth of the Ice Fjord). 418 m. Air $t^0 = 2.5$ C. Obs. P. H.				
0	B.	2.73	31.83	25.40
10	P.-N.	2.21	32.31	25.83
20	»	2.00	32.51	25.00
30	»	1.45	32.80	26.27
50	»	0.98	33.98	27.25
75	»	0.84	33 51 (?)	[26.82]
100	»	0.52	34.50	27 60
150	»	1.79	34.74	27.81
200	»	1.40	34 73	27 83
300	»	2.45	34.86	27.86
400	»	2.71	34.96	27.91

Depth Metres	Instrument	t^0 C.	S $^0/_{00}$	σ_t
\multicolumn{5}{c}{Stat. 31. 6. IX. 1910 (6.30—7.15 a. m.)}				
\multicolumn{5}{c}{78° 4' N., 11° 15' E. 235 m. Air $t^0 = 2.0$° C. Obs. A. H.}				
0	B.	2.14	32.29	25.81
10	P.-N.	3.09	32.50	25.90
20	»	3.18	33.93	27.02
30	»	2.37	34.47	27.54
50	»	2.23	34.62	27.07
75	»	2.40	34.79	27.79
100	»	2.48	34.75	27.76
150	»	2.95	34.94	27.87
200	»	2.83	34.95	27.89
220	»	2.73	34.97	27.92
\multicolumn{5}{c}{Stat. 30. 6. IX. 1910 (9.30—10.15 a. m.)}				
\multicolumn{5}{c}{78° 5' N., 10° 0' E. 195 m. Air $t^0 = 4.1$° C. Obs. P.-H.}				
0	B.	2.98	32.59	25.99
10	P.-N.	2.85	32.68	26.07
20	»	2.83	33.29	26.47
30	»	2.23	34.37	27.47
50	»	3.21	34.79	27.72
75	»	4.45	35.04	27.79
100	»	4.22	35.01	27.80
150	»	3.63	34.97	27.83
180	»	3.15	34.97	27.88
\multicolumn{5}{c}{Stat. 29. 6. IX. 1910 (11.30 a. m. 1.45 p. m.)}				
\multicolumn{5}{c}{78° 1' N., 9° 10' E. 1070 m. Air $t^0 = 4.1$° C. Obs. P.-H.}				
0	B.	3.93	33.35	26.51
10	P.-N.	3.91	33.47	26.59
20	»	5.43	34.73	27.44
30	»	5.08	34.97	27.59
50	»	5.04	35.02	27.71
75	»	4.56	35.07	27.81
100	»	4.23	35.07	27.84
150	»	3.79	35.06	27.89
200	»	3.40	35.09	27.95
300	»	2.84	35.07	27.99
400	»	2.77	35.03	27.97
500	E.	1.62	34.91	27.90
600	»	0.82	34.92	28.02
800	»	− 0.44	{ 34.92 { 34.91	28.08 28.08
1000	»	1.07	{ 34.80 { 34.90	28.09 28.09

Depth Metres	Instrument	t^0 C.	$S^0{}_{00}$	σ_t
		Stat. 4. 7. IX. 1910 (11.30 a. m. 1.0 p. m.)		
		75° 11' N., 10° 40' E. Air $t^0 = 5.0°$ C. Obs. A. H.		
0	B.	5.90	34.97	27.50
20	P.-N.	5.94	34.99	27.58
50	»	5.10	35.00	27.74
75	»	4.50	35.05	27.79
100	»	4.10	35.06	27.83
»	»	4.05	35.04	27.84
200	»	3.40	35.00	27.92
400	»	2.49	35.01	27.97
600	E.	1.80	34.96	27.99
800	»	0.14	34.87	28.02
1000	»	− 0.48	34.85	28.03
		Stat. 3. 7. IX. 1910 (7.30 p. m.)		
		74° 55' N., 13° 40' E. Air $t^0 = 4.2°$ C. Obs. P.-H.		
0	B.	6.25	34.56	27.20
10	P.-N.	6.58	34.68	27.26
20	»	6.48	34.66	27.25
30	»	6.43	34.79	27.36
50	»	6.33	35.08	27.59
75	»	5.95	35.00	27.63
100	»	5.77	35.08	27.67
150	»	5.05	35.04	27.73
200	»	4.40	35.08	27.83
300	»	3.79	35.04	27.87
400	E.	2.70	34.99	27.94
600	»	1.02	34.91	27.96
800	»	0.29	{34.92 / 34.94}	28.05 / 28.07
1200	»	− 0.77	{34.93 / 34.92}	28.11 / 28.10
1500	»	− 0.97	{34.88 / 34.87}	28.07 / 28.07

TABLE II

gives observations of Temperature, Salinity, and Density at the Sea-Surface.

Station	Date and Hour l. t.			Latitude		Longitude		t^0 C.	$S\ ^0/_{00}$	σ_t
	June, 1910			N		E				
1	25			$74^0\ 40'$		$10^0\ 10'$		4.03	34.01	27.74
	-							5.07	35.06	27.07
2	-			- 52		15 5		5.38	35.08	27.72
	-	N		- 59		14 25		5.43	35.08	27.71
3	-			- 55		13 40		4.83	35.03	27.74
	-	4	p. m.	75 1		- 4		4.58	35.06	27.79
4	-			- 8		11 20		4.49	35.00	27.83
	-	10	—	- 13		10 15		4.58	35.07	27.80
	-	M		- 17		9 54		4.18	35.07	27.85
	26	2	a. m.	- 22		- 2		3.81	35.05	27.87
	-	4	—	- 26		8 11		4.37	35.00	27.77
5	-			- 28		7 40		3.93	35.05	27.80
	-	8		- 36		6 11		4.38	35.00	27.82
	-	10		- 42		5 13		3.73	34.90	27.81
	-	N		- 48		4 45		3.93	35.01	27.83
6	-			- 45		- 20		4.18	34.97	27.77
	-	8	p. m.	- 51		5 1		3.48	34.97	27.84
	-	10	—	- 53		- 12		4.18	35.00	27.84
	-	M		- 55		0 24		4.23	35.01	27.80
	27	2	a. m.	- 57		7 8		1.58	35.05	27.79
7	-			- 57		- 30		1.43	35.08	27.83
	-	6	—	76 0		8 11		4.23	35.00	27.83
	-	8	—	- 2		- 48		4.38	35.00	27.81
8	-			- 0		9 45		4.39	34.97	27.75
	-	N		- 7		10 10		4.43	35.08	27.83
	-	2	p. m.	- 10		- 55		4.43	35.01	27.77
9	-			- 11		11 15		4.23	34.54	27.42
	-	4	—	- 13		- 39		4.21	34.57	27.45
10	-			- 16		12 30		4.32	34.79	27.01
	-	8	—	- 19		13 8		4.40	34.94	27.72
	-	9		- 21		- 27		5.38	34.88	27.56
11	-			- 20		13 45		4.03	34.70	27.50
	-	M		- 29		- 28		4.51	34.88	27.66
	28	1	a. m.	- 33		- 4		5.08	34.02	27.03
	-	2	—	- 38		12 39		3.57	33.95	27.01
	-	3	—	- 43		- 15		4.08	34.70	27.54

Station	Date and Hour l. t.			Latitude	Longitude	t^0 C.	$S^0/_{00}$	σ_t
	June, 1910			N	E			
	28	4	a. m.	76° 48'	11° 59'	3.30	33.87	26.97
	-	5	—	- 53	- 43	3.98	33.91	26.95
12	-			- 50	- 0	4.20	33.92	26.93
	-					2.68	33.53	26.77
13	-			77 2	12 21	3.39	33.35	26.55
	-	10	a. m.	- 12	- 23	3.90	33.74	26.82
14	-			- 10	13 5	3.32	33.95	27.04
	-	1	p. m.	- 22	12 45	4.93	33.99	26.91
	-	2	—	- 28	- 44	4.83	34.08	26.99
	-	3	—	- 34	- 44	4.38	34.09	27.04
	-	4	—	- 41	- 43	5.23	34.08	26.94
	-	5	—	- 47	- 30	5.39	33.96	26.82
	-	6	—	- 52	- 21	5.18	34.06	26.93
	-	7	—	- 58	- 0	5.59	34.22	27.00
	-	8	—	78 3	11 51	0.49	33.82	26.59
	-	9	—	- 8	- 30	5.93	33.77	26.61
	-	10	—	- 14	- 21	5.83	33.46	26.37
	-	11	—	- 19	- 0	5.71	33.60	26.51
	-	M		- 24	10 53	5.93	33.06	26.52
	29	1	a. m.	- 24	- 53	5.23	33.75	26.68
	-	2	—	- 24	- 53	4.59	33.85	26.83
	-	3	—	- 36	- 28	4.39	33.84	26.84
	-	4	—	- 48	- 2	4.10	33.95	26.95
	-	8	—	- 30	- 32	4.73	34.88	27.63
	July, 1910							
	17	4	p. m.			0.28	34.36	27.03
	-	5	—			0.18	34.34	27.03
17	-			- 53	7 20	0.03	34.17	26.91
	-	9	—	- 50	6	0.48	34.33	26.98
	-	10	—	- 47	0 48	0.03	34.01	27.18
	-	11	—	- 44	- 20	0.63	34.43	27.04
	-	M		- 42	5 52	0.49	34.73	27.30
18	18			- 40	- 2	0.43	34.70	27.34
	-	3.30 a. m.		- 37	4 56	5.08	34.16	27.02
	-	5	—	- 32	- 25	5.33	34.29	27.09
	-	6.30	—	- 28	3 54	5.83	34.90	27.59
19	-			- 27	2 43	0.08	34.95	27.53
	-	10	—	- 21	- 42	5.10	34.52	27.29
	-	11.30	—	- 17	1 39	5.08	34.73	27.48
	-	1 p. m.		- 14	0 49	4.93	34.32	27.17
20	-			- 14	- 24	4.43	33.67	26.70

Station	Date and Hour l. t.	Latitude	Longitude	t^0 C.	$S^0/_{00}$	σ_t
	July, 1910	N	W			
	18 5.30 p. m.	78° 9'	0° 22'	3.08	33.45	26.66
21	-	- 8	- 35	2.73	33.36	26.02
	19 10.30 a. m.	77 50	- 43	4.30	33.70	26.73
	- N	- 52	- 27	3.08	33 53	26.72
	- 1.30 p. m.	- 45	- 20	3.58	33.65	26.77
22	-	- 41	- 22	4.38	33.71	26.74
	- 7 —	- 32	- 33	4.33	34.72	27.56
	- 8.30 p. m.	- 23	- 44	4.33	34.03	27.00
23	-	- 15	- 35	4.08	33.02	26.94
	20 2 a. m.	- 18	- 27	4.48	34.43	27.30
	- 3.30 —	- 19	- 37	4.58	34.46	27.32
			E.			
	- 5 —	- 21	0 18	4.43	34 40	27.33
	- 6.30 —	- 22	- 40	4 48	34 34	27.23
	- 8 —	- 25	1 12	4 33	34.45	27.34
24	-	- 22	- 23	4.08	34.52	27.41
	- 2 p. m.	- 28	- 47	5.08	34.89	27.61
	- 3.30 —	- 30	2 17	5 73	35.08	27.67
	- 5 —	- 33	- 48	6.18	34.94	27.51
25	-	- 29	4 11	5.68	34.94	27.57
	21 2 a. m.	- 44	- 3	5.73	34.91	27.54
	- 4 —	- 48	- 25	5.83	34.94	27.55
26	22	- 43	5 15	5.68	34.88	27.53
	- 7 a. m.	- 45	- 40	5.73	34.92	27.55
	- 8.30 —	- 48	0 23	5 06	34.89	27.50
	- 10 —	- 51	- 58	5.88	34.94	27.55
27	-	- 53	7 21	6.23	34.88	27.46
28	-	- 57	8 32	0.90	34 08	27.44
29	-	78 1	9 10	6.93	34.79	27.29
30	-	- 5	10 0	6.43	34.73	27.31
31	23	- 0	11 0	5.18	32.84	25.07
	August, 1910					
32	8		Bock Bay	5.23		
33	19	79 44	10 25	3.49	33.80	26.97
34	-	- 52	9 45	2.03	33.02	26.81
35	-	80 0	8 55	1 38	32.91	26.36
36	-	79 29	9 30	4.48	33.70	26.72
37	-	- 33	8 10	3.04	33.50	26.70
38	26	- 50	12 5	3 20	34.31	27.34
39	-	80 1	- 5	3.03	34.24	27.30
40	-	- 6	- 4	2.88	34.16	27.25

Station	Date and Hour l. t.	Latitude	Longitude	t^0 C.	$S \, ^0/_{00}$	σ_t
	September, 1910	N	E			
41	6	Mouth of Ice Fjord		2.73	31.83	25.40
	- 4 a. m.	78° 8'	12° 57'	2.39	32.05	25.60
	- 5 -	- 7	- 19	2.37	31.73	25.34
	- 6 -	- 0	11 40	2 37	31.85	25.44
31	-	- 4	- 15	2.14	32.29	25.81
	- 8.15 -	- 0	10 45	2 03	32.59	26.00
	- 9.15 -	- 8	- 13	2.00	32.00	26.05
30	-	- 5	- 00	2.98	32.50	25.99
29	-	- 1	9 10	3.03	33 35	26.51
	- 3 p. m.	77 57	8 44	3.18	32.84	26.17
	- 4 -	- 51	- 32	4.53	33.78	26.78
	- 6 -	- 30	- 10	4 50	33.74	26.75
	- 8 -	- 21	- 21	4.33	33.57	26.63
	- 10 -	- 4	- 38	3.83	33.64	26.75
	- M	76 48	- 55	3.96	33.29	26.45
	7 2 a. m.	- 32	9 12	4.23	34.17	27.13
	- 4 -	- 15	- 30	4.73	34.14	27.05
	- 5 -	- 7	- 38	5 58	34.91	27.56
	- 6 -	75 59	- 47	5.03	35.01	27.63
	- 7 -	- 51	- 55	5 78	35.00	27.65
	- 8 -	- 42	10 4	5.78	35.02	27.62
	- 10 -	- 26	- 21	5.81	34.80	27.45
4		- 11	- 40	5.96	34.97	27.56
	- 2 p. m.	- 11	11 3	5.76	34.74	27.41
	- 4 -	- 4	12 2	5.03	34.70	27.39
	- 6 p. m.	74 58	13 1	6.09	35.06	27.01
3	-	- 55	- 40	6.25	34.56	27.20
	- 11 -	- 42	14 0	6.22	34.87	27.45
	- M	- 34	- 21	6.42	34.98	27.51
	8 1 a. m.	- 27	- 30	6.95	35.08	27.51
	- 2 -	- 19	- 52	6.79	35.00	27.52
	- 3 -	- 12	15 7	6.88	35.09	27.53
	- 4 -	- 5	- 22	7.30	34.96	27.36
	- 5 -	73 57	- 37	7.27	34.97	27.38
	- 6 -	- 50	- 53	7.20	34.00	27.37
	- 7 -	- 42	16 8	6.17	34.87	27.40
	- 8 -	- 35	- 23	7.07	34.88	27.34
	- 9 -	- 28	- 38	7.22	34.88	27.32
	- 10 -	- 20	- 51	7.66	34 01	27 28
	- 11 -	- 14	17 2	7.75	34.95	27 30

Station	Date and Hour l. t.	Latitude	Longitude	t^0 C.	$S\,^0/_{00}$	σ_t
	September, 1910	N	E			
	8 N	73^0 7'	17^0 10'	8.04	34.91	27.22
	- 1 p. m.	72 59	- 20	8.08	34.83	27.16
	- 2 —	- 51	30	7.86	34.87	27.21
	- 3 —	- 43	- 40	7.87	34.88	27.22
	- 4 —	- 36	- 50	7.02	34.90	27.24
	- 5 —	- 28	18 1	8.10	34.88	27.19
	- 6 —	- 20	- 11	7.87	34.80	27.24
	- 7 —	- 12	- 21	7.77	34.88	27.24
	- 8 —	- 4	- 31	7.82	34.87	27.22
	- 9 —	71 57	- 40	7.86	34.82	27.18
	- 10 —	- 50	- 49	7.83	34.70	27.16
	- 11 p. m.	- 42	- 58	7.22	34.70	27.25
-	M	- 35	19 7	7.22	34.83	27.28
9	1 a. m.	- 27	- 17	8.52	34.48	26.80
	- 2 —	- 19	- 26	8.32	34.48	26.83
	- 3 —	- 10	- 36	8.27	34.51	26.87
	- 4 —	- 2	- 46	8.47	34.47	26.81
	- 5 —	70 56	- 51	8.62	34.26	26.61
	- 6 —	- 49	- 57	8.77	34.30	26.62
	- 7 —	- 42	20 2	8.82	34.22	26.55
	- 8 —	- 36	- 8	8.82	34.17	26.52
	- 9 —	- 29	- 13	8.82	34.14	26.50
	- 10 —	- 23	- 19	8.72	34.12	26.49
	- 11 —	- 16	- 24	7.92	34.26	26.72
-	N	Fuglo to Tromso		8.22	34.17	26.01
	- 1 p. m.	— · —		7.97	34.15	26.63
	- 2 —	— · —		7.82	34.15	26.65
	- 3 —	— · —		8.09	33.97	26.48
	- 4 —	— · —		8.22	34.14	26.60

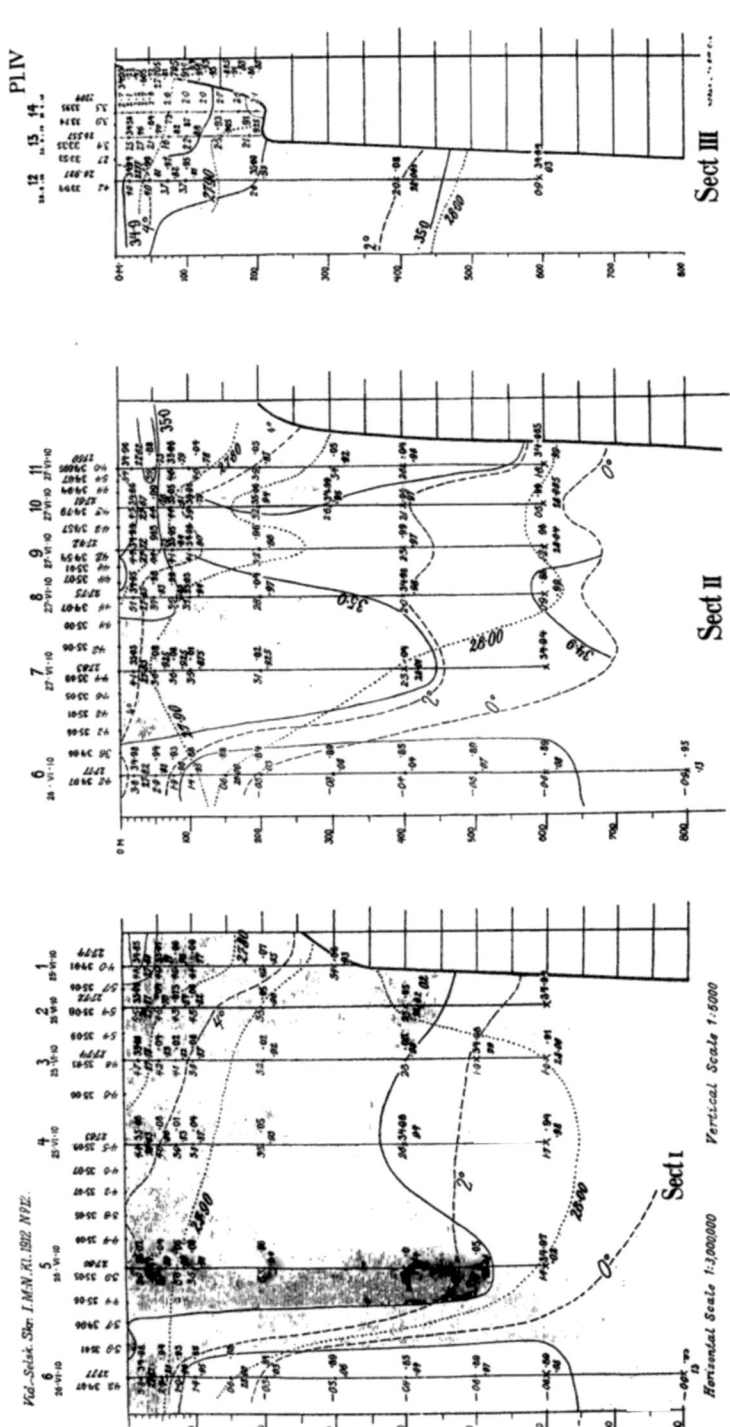

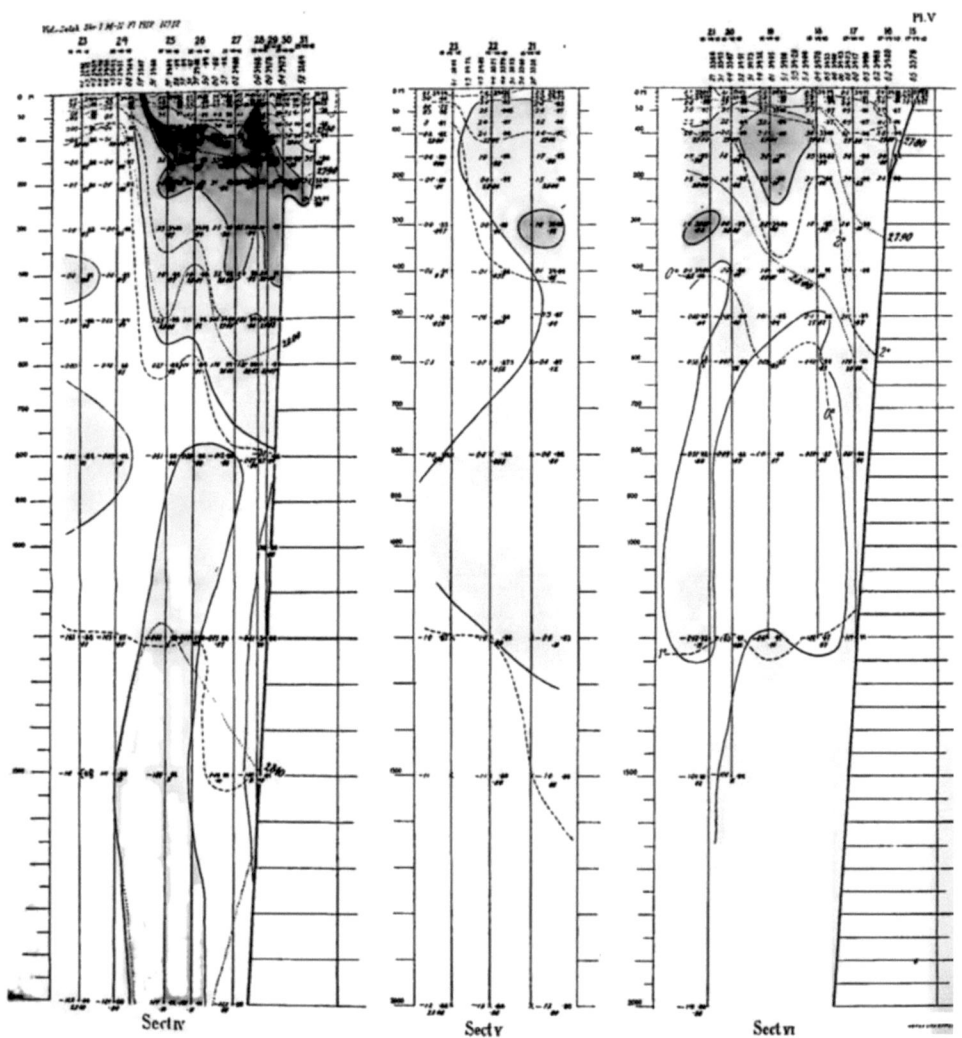

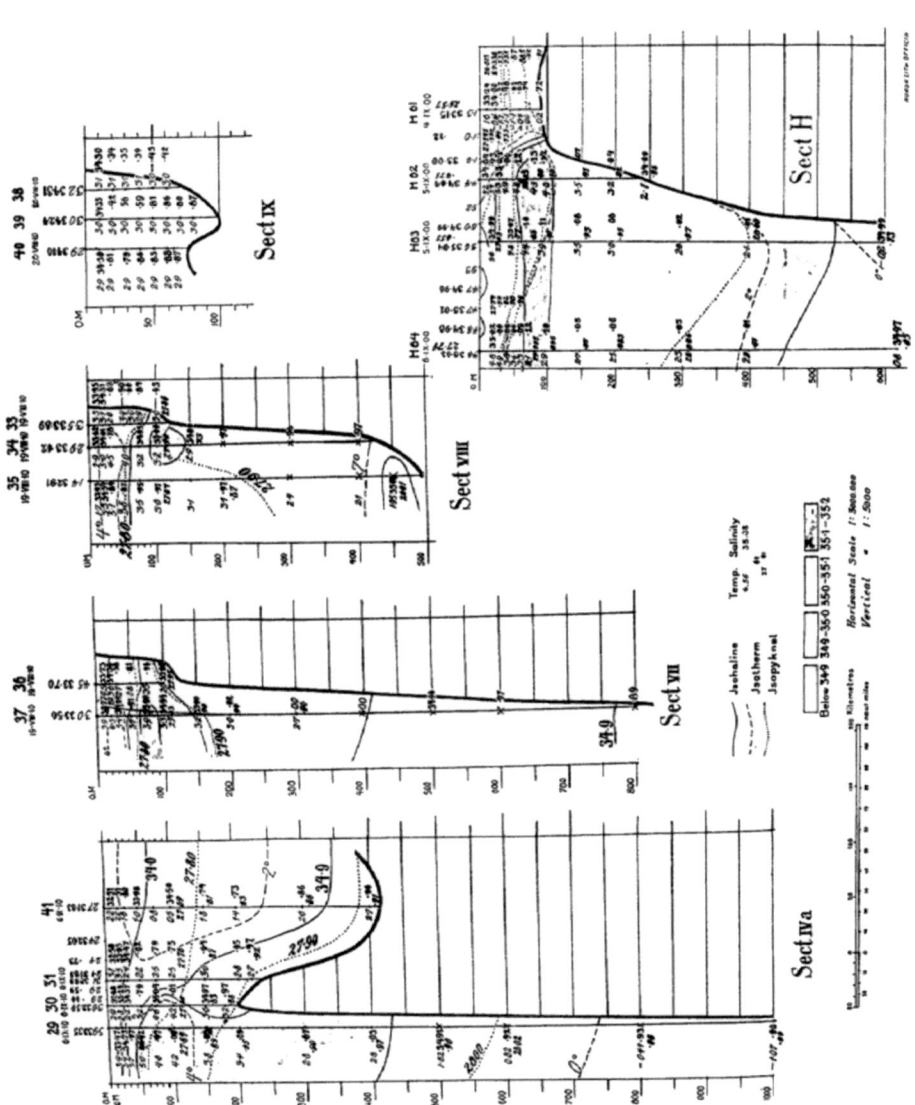